argonaut

pocket
guide

CRETE

GW00725500

Copyright © 1984 by P. Efstathiadis & Sons S.A.
All rights reserved.

ISBN 960 226 057 2

Photography by M. Granitsas

Designed by Dora Lelouda

Distributed by:
P. Efstathiadis & Sons S.A.
Ag. Athanasiou Str. GR. 145 65 Anixi Attikis Tel. 8131593
14 Valtetsiou St. GR. 106 80 Athens Tel. 3615011
34 Olympou-Diikitiriou St. GR. 546 30 Thessaloniki Tel. 511781

EFSTATHIADIS GROUP
Agiou Athanasiou St. Anixi Attikis, Tel. 8131593
14 Valtetsiou St. Athens, Tel. 3615011

CRETE

by R. Archer

EFSTATHIADIS GROUP

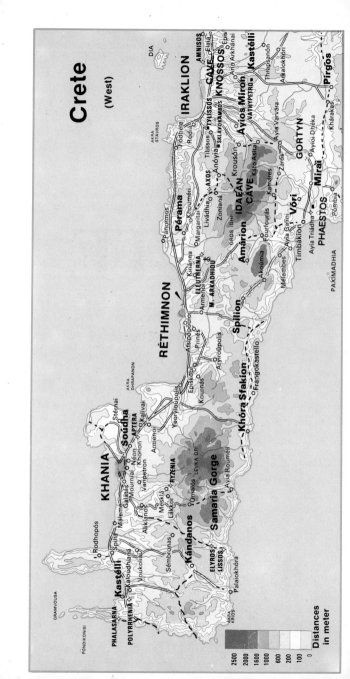

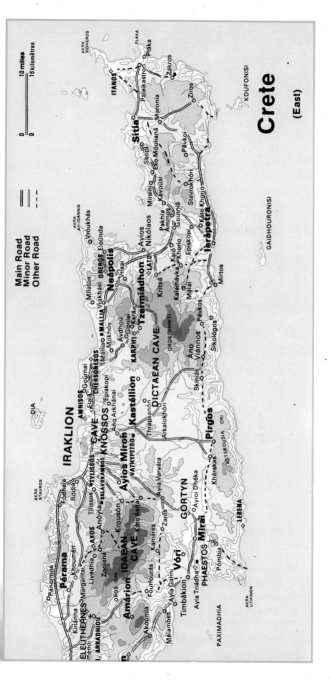

Crete
(East)

Main Road
Minor Road
Other Road

0   10 miles
0   16 kilomètres

CONTENTS

3 Everyday Pleasures

4 Traveling to Crete

5 Traveling around Crete

6 When to go

7 General Practical Information from A to Z

8 A little Greek for travelers

Istrou bay (near St. Nicholas)

1. Preface

CRETE: THE GREAT ISLAND

Crete: what varied images, how many different associations this blunt word evokes in many people. For some, Crete is the homeland of an ancient civilization, **the Minoans,** and thus a place of archaeological sites and museums with works of art. For others, Crete is an island of sunshine and beaches, and thus a place for escaping history, past and present. Then for some, Crete is a land of villages and tavernas, a place to meet the local inhabitants and to enjoy new ways of living. For still others, Crete is a land of rugged mountains and trails and caves, a natural preserve to walk about and explore. And this does not exhaust the associations of Crete. There is the Crete of **medieval Christian chapels,** for instance, with fine old **Byzantine frescoes** and **ikons.** There is a Crete rich in dances and music and folklore and traditional festivities. There is also a Crete with modern resort facilities, fine restaurants, shops with a variety of gifts and souvenirs.

But the point is clear. Crete is all these places–and more. (There is, for instance, a Crete of surprises–an island with **Venetian remains** and **Turkish remains,** not to mention **Roman remains**). Crete's strength, its appeal, is this diversity. It is an island where everyone can find something to enjoy. Indeed, perhaps no similarly sized place in the whole world offers so many contrasts, so many possibilities, so many different significances and so many varied diversions, as does Crete.

This is the Crete that attracts so many visitors each year, and it is the Crete that will be conveyed in this guide. It is a place so many-layered, so diverse, so full of unexpected experiences, that the first-time visitor can not be expected to be aware of all the possibilities. Such a guide should at least increase the chances of discovering more of them. And even those who return to Crete for another visit, or even for several visits, might well be reminded of how much more remains to be discovered.

For one thing, Crete – despite its sense of tradition and its image of persistence – is a place that seems constantly to be changing. The landscape itself changes from season to season-flowers come and go, the mountains change their coloring, even the atmosphere changes. A visit to Crete in the winter will reveal a surprisingly different island from the one seen in the summer.

Of course the touristic facilities change – from year to year and then throughout the year. The general trend has been toward more elaborate facilities – and many more facilities. But what is important is that, generally speaking, the island has been able to absorb these many new facilities. Here and there some large resorts or large numbers of tourists may seem to put too much pressure on the island. But those who are bothered by this can simply move on-and before you know it, the landscape will have changed and you can see a farmer astride his donkey going off to work in the fields.

11

Even the archaeological remains do not escape change. Not only are new sites continually being discovered, many of the older sites are being reworked. Often the new excavations extend both the time and the area of the earlier Cretans, thus forcing reappraisals of many earlier finds and ideas. Archaeology on Crete is still a very dynamic activity, and even those visitors who are not primarily interested in this aspect of the island should gain some sense of the exciting new work that is still underway.

And then there are the people of Crete, the present inhabitants. Some of them in more remote villages seem to have changed little. Yet the Cretans most foreigners will encounter seem to have rushed into the contemporary world. And when Cretans do anything, they do it wholeheartedly, intensely. It is the spirit that has become internationally associated with the name "Zorba" (although ironically, Zorba himself was not a Cretan)-a passionate embracing of life. Not all visitors to Crete will have the opportunity to encounter such intense Cretans, but everyone should be aware that there is this side to Cretans.

For Crete is much more than just another holiday island or historical realm. It is a very special place, perhaps unique. There will always be parts of Crete that baffle some visitors, elude some, even frustrate some. It is not a simple "quaint" little island. Even Greeks themselves will admit that the Cretans are different. That is why Crete is known traditionally among Greeks as "the Great Island"–

in reference to far more tha its physical dimensions. It is tribute to the richness, th diversity, the intensity, of thi place. Foreigners cannot ex pect to experience all this "greatness", but this guid should help visitors be mor aware of the many possibilitie of Crete.

THE LAND AND ITS LIFE

No matter how one arrives or **Crete**, no matter how ofter one returns, no matter wha one's motives for coming, the first strong impact comes from the island's physical features its terrain and its life forms. I can be quite awesome, whether standing on the deck of ar approaching ship or looking down from an arriving airplane, to view the raw mountainous form of Crete rising from the **Mediterranean.**

Yet **Crete** is not actually that large, even as islands go. Although the fifth largest in the **Mediterranean** (after **Sicily, Sardinia, Cyprus,** and **Corsica**), Crete is only some 8,260 sq. km.-about the area of **Puerto Rico** or **Jamaica** or **Cape Breton Island** (itself but part of **Nova Scotia**). Crete is some 260 km. long, some 60 km. at its widest and only about 12 km. at its narrowest. This means that you are never more than about 30 km. from the coast, although curving roads may stretch out the actual route. And the coastline, because of the many indentations and projections, comes to about 1,100 km. All the good harbors are along the north coast, while good swimming beaches are apt to be found at almost any point around the island.

Undoubtedly, the predominant physical feature of Crete are its mountains. For the most part they are limestone, formed during the **Tertiary and Cretaceous Periods** many millions of years ago when a great sea lay over this region and then were forced upwards by the thrust of the great moving plates. Crete, in fact, its almost along the edge of where the plate moving up from Africa meets the plate from Europe, and this accounts for its somewhat unstable state-and thus the occasional minor tremors. But it is not volcanic, and no one has lost a life from an earthquake in living memory.

Seen from a distant perspective, the mountains of Crete might appear as one unbroken chain, but they are divided into four major ranges by all who live on their slopes. At the far east are the **Sitia Mountains;** just west of these are the **Dhikti,** or **Lasithi, Mountains;** then, more or less extending over central Crete is the **Psiloritis Range,** traditionally known as the **Idha Range;** while western Crete is pretty much dominted by the **White Mountains.** The two rival high points are **Timios Stavros** of the **Idha Range,** at 2,456 meters, and **Pachnes** of the **White Mountains,** at 2,452 meters.

These are hardly among the highest peaks of the world's mountains, but whatever they lack in height the mountains of Crete make up for in their rugged grandeur and constant presence. There is snow on some of the peaks and slopes well into the early summer so that the visitor may enjoy that special thrill of being in a hot Mediterranean city and looking up and beyond to white-topped mountains.

Crete's mountains are distinguished by other features, too. Because they are principally limestone, they are filled with caves: of the approximately 6,200 known caves of all Greece, 3,200 are said to be on Crete. (Several of these caves feature in Crete's myths and legends and history and will be discussed under the appropriate excursions). Then there are the various gorges or ravines and passes that cut through the mountains; the most notable one, the **Samaria Gorge,** is one of the major attractions of Crete and will be described in detail as an excursion. Another variation in the rough terrain are the several large upland basins-almost stadium-like in their symmetry and with their surrounding slopes. (These, too, will be discussed under their appropriate excursions.)

In fact, most visitors to Crete spend most of their time along the several coastal plains and view the mountains in the distance or as terrain to be crossed. There is also the one large plain at sea level, the **Messara,** about 32 km. long and some 5 km. wide, extending on an east-west axis in the central part of Crete, just up from the south coast. This, too, will be described in more detail as part of one of the major excursions. And if it isn't clear why most visitors today need not spend that much time in Crete's mountains, it is because the Minoans didn't, either: the Minoans, except for certain sacred peaks and caves-and for a few exceptional "retreat" settlements-did not choose to live in the mountains. The Minoans' 13 idea of "the good life" may not have been exactly the same as that of the modern holiday visitor to Crete, but they all share a sense that life was better close to the coast and where the vegetation thrives.

Many of Crete's mountainous slopes are now barren limestone as a result of millenniums of deforestation. This undoubtedly began in the ancient world, when the land was stripped by those seeking wood for charcoal burning or for buildings and ships; uncontrolled grazing by sheep and goats finished the job. That said, there are many more forested areas than is sometimes suggested, far more green and diverse vegetation than is commonly admitted. Pine, cypress, oak, the ilex tree, chestnut trees-they are found in various stands. And of course there are the countless olive trees: actually, someone once claimed to have counted thirteen million of them, and in recent years there has been considerable new planting of olive trees. Likewise of the orange trees. And one tree that many people may not recognize is the carob, a smallish evergreen that produces longish pods like big green beans; the carob is rich in sugar (it is used as a substitute for chocolate) while its pods are used for various manufacturing processes. The carob is sometimes known as **"St. John's bread,"** in allusion to the food that **John the Baptist** ate in the wilderness, and some people still enjoy chewing the dried carob.

Crete also has many almond trees, not to mention various fruit trees-peaches, apricots, cherries, even some bananas. The mulberry tree is to be seen-as late as the 19th century there was a modest silk industry on Crete. But there is no denying that the prime cultivated plant on Crete today is the vine. The varieties of grapes are used in three ways: the **rosaki** is the favored table grape; the **sultani** is used for making raisins; and other varieties are used for making wines. The table grapes can be enjoyed during a limited season, when they are virtually thrust on every passerby. The raisins are often treated in the opposite manner: held back by families in hopes of getting a better price when the world market changes. (Incidentally, the production of raisins dates primarily from the 1920s, when Greeks from Turkey were exchanged for Turks then living on Crete.) As for the wines, they are hardly of vintage class, but the better ones may be drunk around the year and every year as quite acceptable accompaniments to the Cretan cuisine.

But what really makes Crete a naturalist's paradise are its many wildflowers. There are about 1,500 known species or varieties, and over 100 of these are found only on Crete. There are many orchids, for instance, and irises; there is cyclamen and rock roses and lupins and arums and anemones. There are also the many reason's Cretan mountain men traditionally wore high boots. And there are the various herbs; in particular, the Cretan dittany, **Origanum dictamnus,** a member of the mint family, that is used in seasoning foods and in an herb tea. The Cretans prize it as a medicinal plant, especially for giving comfort to women in childbirth. Those who enjoy tracking down and

14

identifying wild flowers had best bring their own special knowledge or guidebooks, because the subject could hardly be begun in a short guide such as this.

Fauna, however, is a subject more easily exhausted. Although such wild animals as the badger, hedgehog, hare, rabbit, marten, weasel, and even a wildcat have been reported even in recent years, the visitor will not likely see any of these. There are a few snakes, but no poisonous ones. There are non-poisonous scorpions, and one rare poisonous spider. Crete's relatively few year-round rivers and its one small freshwater lake are not known to support any fishlife. There are bats and butterflies and many insects, of course. But the one truly distinctive animal on Crete is a wild goat with the scientific name of **Capra aegagrus creticus**-this signifying that it is a subspecies related to the wild goat found over in the **Caucasus** and down into **Iran** and **Pakistan.** Almost certainly it was isolated on Crete many hundreds of thousands of years ago when Crete became cut off from the mainland of Asia Minor. (A dwarf hippopotamus was also left stranded on Crete, but it long ago became extinct.) The Cretan wild goat-known locally as **kri-kri,** or **agrimi**-may weigh up to 45 kilos and the record horn spread is some 78 cm. Several decades ago it was realized that it was in danger of becoming extinct, so hunting was prohibited and as many individuals as possible were taken to three islet-sanctuaries along the north coast of Crete;

Lasithi Wind mills

the population has now been brought back to the extent that they are being released in the Cretan wilds (and in recent years the government has even allowed people to hunt the goat on the main islet preserve, **Dia,** off **Iraklion**: but it is very expensive, and the goats hardly have a sporting chance).

Most visitors to Crete will never get a chance to see this wild goat (unless they obtain special permission to visit one of the islet sanctuaries). But what everyone may enjoy are the birds of Crete. There are many species of both resident and migrant birds: warblers, goldfinches, hoopoes, shrikes, egrets, buntings, kestrels, bee-eaters, larks, the griffon vulture, the booted eagle, night-herons, and many more. Studies in recent years have confirmed that vast numbers and many species of birds migrating between Europe and

Picking grapes (Archanes)

Africa put down for brief stops on Crete. As with wild flowers, those who enjoy tracking down and identifying birds must bring their own knowledge and field-guides.

Everyone, however, can enjoy the superb vistas of Crete, the sunrises and sunsets, the brooding mountains, the harsh dignity of certain landscapes. One need not know their names to enjoy the wildflowers or the birds. Whether you come seeking a natural background to a holiday or a natural retreat for your special enthusiasms, whether you want to capture it with your camera or simply remember it in your mind's eye, Crete is a land that demands respect and repays attention.

THE HISTORICAL BACKGROUND

Many people-even those who intend only to relax in the sun-come to Crete knowing one thing about its history: There were a people called **Minoans** who long ago had a luxurious and influential civilization based at **Knossos**. If pressed, most people can list a few details of this Minoan culture— bull-leapers and bare-breasted snake goddesses and fine ceramics and labyrinthine palaces. But what most people end up discovering on Crete is that there is so much more to the island's history, not only many more extensive phases but many other fascinating details. Just as there is more than one Crete that attracts visitors, there is more than one layer to Crete's history. Even those not interested in "old stones" or historical details will appreciate the significance of the background against which they spend their Cretan holiday.

THE PRE-MINOAN CRETE
(6500 - 2600 B.C.)

Although Crete had probably been attached to the mainland of Asia Minor and Greece up till about one million years ago, there has never been any indication that human beings were present that early. But it has been established that the first human beings arrived by about 6.500 B.C. Exactly who these people were-where they came from-what language they spoke—none of this has been established. But it is generally agreed that they came from Asia Minor, possibly from further down along the **Mediterranean coast,** and maybe even from Egypt. In any case, they did not all come at once; there must certainly have been successive waves over several thousand years. These immigrants brought what is known as the "neolithic culture" with them— pottery, tools, domesticated animals, cultivated crops, weaving. (Visitors to Crete will see some of this **Neolithic culture** in the **Iraklion Museum's** displays.)

EARLY MINOAN PERIOD
(2600 - 200 B.C.)

Life went on in a relatively changeless, faceless way until sometime between about 3.000 and 2.600 B.C. when a new wave or waves of immigrants

A branch of Olive tree

seem to have brought an extra surge to the cultural development of Crete. This is now considered to have begun the **Minoan culture.** Obviously it did not begin overnight, but against the previous 3.500 to 4.000 years, Minoan culture developed quickly. Probably the people who instigated this surge were also from Asia Minor. Soon they were using copper, decorating their pottery in distinctive styles, carving precious and semiprecious stones, and building ambitious vaulted circular tombs for the burial of their dead. These early Minoans flourished especially around the eastern end of the island and on the **Messara Plain,** but there were also active settlements at **Knossos** and **Phaestos.**

MIDDLE MINOAN PERIOD (2000 - 1550 B.C.)

Then, about 2000 B.C. there occurred another surge in Cretan life. At **Knossos, Phaestos, Mallia,** and **Kato Zakros,** quite ambitious palaces were erected, palaces not necessarily in the sense of royal residences but in the sense of some bases of social and economic power. There is no suggestion of military power, but probably there was no need for it: it was enough to control the agriculture and animal husbandry and crafts and trade. Perhaps it was nothing more than the dynamic and assertive members of Minoan society setting themselves over the more passive and traditional members.

However it came about,

Minoan society entered a new phase. The activity seemed to shift more to central Crete, and at the same time the Minoans began to trade with other peoples as far away as **Troy** and **Italy.** Crete had plentiful cedar and cypress forests to make ships, and by importing raw materials such as tin and copper, the Minoans could make bronze that they then traded at a profit. Minoans also excelled at their elegant jewelry, fine pottery, and in other arts and crafts. They even used a pictographic script for limited purposes, which about 1.700 B.C. was replaced by a more advanced script, now known as **Linear A.** (Although scholars have made various claims as to what language this records, there is no general agreement as to even the roots of the language).

About 1.700, too, the main palaces were struck by a major earthquake. They were quickly rebuilt and at a far grander scale, and Minoan culture seems to have continued virtually uninterrupted. **Knossos**

seems to have assumed a position of control beyond that of the other palace-centers, but there must have been enough prosperity and power for many to share. There were paved roads, fine villas, harbor facilities, and structures of all kinds. There were Minoans trading throughout much of the then known world. The Minoans continued to make their superb ceramics.

Beyond such tangible achievements, the Minoans seem to have developed a quite elaborate society. Undoubtedly, the mass of people lived a very basic life-with most of them spending most of their time working in the fields. There must have been a class of craftsmen and artisans. There were bureaucrats of one kind or another. And then there was the ruling elite that appears to have recognized the chief of **Knossos** as a sort of **Priest-King. (**In later Greek legend and myth, he was known as **Minos,** but this was probably a title, not a personal name.) And these Minoans

appear to have kept alive their worship of a sort of **Nature Mother Goddess,** who took various forms-such as the well-known **Snake Goddess** - and was accompanied by various symbols, such as the dove and flowers. The bull also played a prominent role in Minoan religious and ceremonial life, and such common symbols as the double axe and horns of consecration were evidently linked with the sacred bull. Whether there were individuals who literally leapt or somersaulted over the horns of charging bulls is still disputed, but there are certainly many representations of this feat in Minoan works.

LATE MINOAN PERIOD (1550 - 1100 B.C.)

About 1.550 or 1.500 B.C. certain stylistic changes in Minoan art and various other developments suggest a new phase in Minoan culture. In particular, about 1.500 B.C. the **Linear A** script was adapted to form a new script, known

as **Linear B**, and since 1.953 this has been known to be recording Greek-an early form, but recognizable Greek. What is more, this same **Linear B** was being used to keep records on the Greek mainland at the centers of the **Mycenaeans,** those early Greeks who had appeared on the mainland about 1.900 B.C. and developed an extensive culture with its center at **Mycenae**. It has thus been generally accepted that these **Mycenaean Greeks** must have somehow begun to exercise some control over the Minoans-at least at the Palace of Knossos.

Then, about 1475 B.C. some major catastrophe seems to have struck **Knossos** and most of the other bases of Minoan culture-the other palaces, villas, harbor towns, and all. Once more, there is little agreement among the scholars as to what this was, although an earthquake accompanied by fire seems as plausible an explanation as any. In recent years there has been an attempt to link this catastrophe with the explosion of the volcanic island of **Santorini** (or **Thera**), some 100 km. north of Crete; quite aside from accompanying earthquakes and any rain of volcanic matter, there would have been a powerful tidal wave.

Whatever the cause, Minoan civilization was severely disrupted at this time but by no means obliterated. Knossos seems to have recovered fairly quickly and there was activity at other traditional Minoan centers. Then about 1375 the palace of Knossos was destroyed by yet another catastrophe. Again, scholars differ as to how thorough this destruction was, but certainly Knos-

sos and the Minoans would never recover any of their former power or glory. The Mycenaeans, meanwhile, had usurped the role of the Minoans around the Mediterranean. It was these **Mycenaean Greeks** who launched some sort. of punitive expedition against **Troy**-what the world has ever since known as the **Trojan War.** Cretans did not feature prominently in it, but **King Idomeneus** led a Cretan contingent there.

POST-MINOAN DARK AGE REVIVAL (1100-500 B.C.)

The Trojan War has been placed by scholars anywhere from 1.250 to 1.150 B.C. And sometime during this period, a new people seem to have been moving down into Greece-the **Dorians**. Actually a Greek-speaking people and as such "cousins" of the **Mycenaeans,** the Dorians appear to have come down from north of Greece and taken over many of the Mycenaean centers. They also appeared on Crete by or shortly after 1.100 B.C., and some Minoans took to living in more remote settlements in the mountains. In general, a "dark age"settled over much of the Aegean world, whether due to some failing in the **Dorian culture** or just some inevitable intermission in the development of civilization. But there was pottery still being made, some of the old sites on Crete remained occupied, and gradually there were new contacts with the kingdoms of the Near East and Egypt. Crete, in fact, became crucial in transmitting certain cultural and artistic elements from these more advanced realms to the Greek world. And the Dorians on Crete, like those at **Sparta,** developed a social system with an elite of warrior-youths raised in communal barracks while the native serfs worked the fields to produce the food. The center of this **Dorian** society on Crete was at **Gortyna,** where its law code remains to this day to astound the visitors.

CLASSICAL-HELLENISTIC CRETE (500-67 B.C.)

The great initiatives, however, were taken by the city-states elsewhere around the Greek world-by the **Ionian Greeks** on the islands off **Turkey,** by such cities as **Corinth** and **Athens.** Yet even though Crete did not participate much in the great golden age of classic Greece, the leading Greek writers and philosophers and historians were frequently paying tribute to Cretan sources and contributions to the mainland culture-especially when it came to sculpture and myths and laws. (Crete played the role in classical Athenian culture that classical Athens was later to play in Roman culture). Somehow the cities on Crete itself never got organized or united, although some did issue their own coins. In the conflicts that swept across the Mediterranean world following the death of **Alexander,** the Cretan cities were able to do little more than try to ally themselves with whoever seemed to be the strongest power of the moment. Crete became knon as the outpost of pirates and as a provider of mercenaries.

ROMAN CRETE (67 B.C.-AD 395)

Off to the west, meanwhile, **Rome** was emerging as the major power and soon moved in on Crete. By 67 B.C., the island was combined with the old Greek colony of **Cyrenaica** (on the coast of North Africa, just south of Crete) to become a **Roman province.** The capital was the old Dorian city of **Gortyna,** but there was an important Roman community at Knossos. The Romans treated Crete as a source of wheat and other raw materials, but they did do a fair amount of building around the island. And as Christianity began to spread through the Roman world, it came early to Crete: the **Apostle Paul,** enroute to Rome about AD 60 is said to have put in along the southern coast of Crete and appointed the first bishop of Crete, **Titus** of **Gortyna. Paul's Epistle** to **Titus** and the spread of Christianity on Crete are among the legacies of this era.

BYZANTINE CRETE (AD 395-1204)

The **Roman Empire** split into western and eastern realms in AD 395, and Crete went with the eastern one with its capital at **Byzantium,** or **Constantinople.** Little was accomplished on Crete during this long "dark age" that settled over much of the known world, and at one point-between 824 and 961-Crete actually came under the control of some **Arab pirates.** The Byzantine Empire made several unsuccessful efforts to regain control, but it was 961 before the **Emperor Nikiphoros Phokas** achieved this goal. Some **Greeks** from 21 the mainland were evidently brought down to revitalize the island.

VENETIAN CRETE
(1204-1669)

Then, in 1.204, a group of Europeans turned aside from what was the **Fourth Crusade** to deliver Jerusalem and instead captured Constantinople. These men, largely French and Italian warrior-knights who became known in Greek history as the **Franks,** divided up the **Byzantine Empire** among themselves, and the **Republic of Venice** was able to "buy" Crete. The Venetians first had to dislodge their rivals, the **Genoese,** from Crete, but by 1.210 the Venetians had established their first Governor of their new colony. Crete's value to the Venetians was originally as a way station for the many Venetian ships that moved throughout the eastern Mediterranean, but very quickly the Venetians saw other possibilities. They brought over Venetian colonists who were invited to exploit the island's potential for producing food and other raw materials. Some Cretan's eventually revolted against the Venetians' rule, but eventually the Venetians won out. And since the Venetians allowed the Greeks to worship in their Orthodox rites, and even encouraged the building and painting of churches, the Cretan's came to accept the Venetian presence.

Meanwhile, the Byzantine Empire - although it had gotten rid of the Frank usurpers-was succumbing to the **Ottoman Turks.** In 1453, **Constantinople** fell to the **Turks** and many Greek scholars and artists fled to Crete. This gave yet another stimulus to life on Crete, and there were a number of churches and monasteries built that reflect the merging of two traditions, Greek Orthodox and Venetian. There was also a revival of literature on Crete, with several poets and dramatists writing in Greek but drawing on Western European traditions. Some Cretan's, too, moved on to **Venice** itself, where they became prominent in early printing ventures and thus contributed to the great **Renaissance.** But perhaps the most notable individual who bridged these two traditions was **Domeniko Theotokopoulos,** a Cretan painter who went to **Venice** and then on to Spain where he attained fame with his distinctive blend of Byzantine and Western painting and called himself **El Greco.**

By the 17th century, the Venetians seemed to be solidly established through Crete. They had great forts in several cities, they were about to build some impressive structures in their capital city, **Candia** (namely, the fountain and the **Loggia** that still surprise visitors), their public and private structures were all over the island. But the Ottoman Turks had slowly been taking over much of the eastern Mediterranean, and by 1.645 they had captured **Khania,** Crete's second largest city. **Rethymnon**-despite its ambitious fort-fel the next year, and in 1.648 the Turks launched their siege of **Candia** (present-day **Iraklion)**

Europe had watched the other outposts of the Christian realm fall to the Turks and now decided to draw the line. But it was too late. Despite please from the Pope and aid

Pithoi (storage jars) in Malllia

A typical cretan

sent by the French king and the Venetians, after 22 years **Candia** fell to the Turks. (The commander of the defense was **Francesco Morosini,** who would soon thereafter gain dubious fame as the commander of the attack on **Athens** that blew up the **Parthenon**).

TURKISH CRETE
(1669-1898)

Many Cretans fled the main cities as they fell to the Turks but other Cretans at first saw the Turks as welcome liberators from the Venetians. All Cretans soon learned that there was no escaping the dead hand of Turkish rule. There was little construction except of mosques and fountains and private homes. Trade and agriculture and crafts remained stagnant-in part because the Turks demanded so much in taxes and tariffs that there was little incentive. The Turks took Cretan youths and raised them as **Janissaries.** And since Christians took the full brunt of the Turkish oppressions, many Cretan "converted" to the Islamic religion. However, as throughout most of the Greek world, the Cretan's kept their Orthodox faith, their Greek language, and their age-old popular cultural traditions alive.

There were also the attempts at throwing off the Turkish rule. The first of the major efforts was in 1.770 when a **Daskaloyiannis** ("John the Lettered One") was to have received help from the **Russians,** who had their own reasons for wanting to undermine the Turks. When the aid failed to appear, Daskaloyiannis offered himself up to the Turks to save his followers; he was flayed alive. (This incident inspired a famous Cretan 23 poem). During the 19th century, there were periodic revolts, including one that Cretans undertook when all Greeks rose up against the Turks starting in 1.821. But when the **new Greek state** was proclaimed in 1.832, with the support of the **Great Powers** of Western Europe, these same powers handed Crete back to the Turks. In 1.866 there was a revolt that saw hundreds of Cretans and Turks killed when the Cretans themselves blew up the powder storeroom at the besieged **Monastery of Arkadhi.** But even this did not move the Great Powers to demand Crete's freedom. It remained until 1.898 when an incident cost the lives of several British soldiers stationed on Crete for the Great Powers to force the Turks to turn over the administration of the island to **Prince George,** younger son of the **King of Greece,** who was to serve as **High Commissioner** of a semi-autonomus Crete.

MODERN CRETE
(1898-Present)

Although there was to be a Cretan assembly and a constitution, many Cretan's still felt this avoided their true goal: **union with Greece.** The leader of this movement was **Eleftherios Venizelos,** born outside **Khania.** He went so far as to call a revolutionary assembly on his own in 1.905, and although he failed to achieve his goal at that time, he did force Prince George out. Venizelos went on to become Premier of Greece, and after a war in the Balkans, Venizelos managed to get Crete finally united with Greece. It was

1.913-the first time that Crete had actually been formally united with the entire Greek community. Venizelos is revered to this day as one of the great sons of Crete.

The next episode that ruffled Crete came in 1.923 when, in the aftermath of the disaster of a Greek military venture in Turkey, the Greeks in Turkey were forced to leave and Turks in Greece were sent back in exchange. Crete's Turkish population left and many Greeks from Asia Minor had to be absorbed on the island. But this was nothing compared to what was to happen in the **Second World War.** As the **Germans** moved swiftly down through the Greek mainland, the **British Commonwealth troops** were forced to retreat to Crete. Thousands of them arrived early in 1.941, but before they could get fully

organized and supplied, the Germans launched an airborne invasion of the island. The first gliders and paratroopers began to descend on Crete on May 20, and Cretans joined the British soldiers in the defense of the island. The Germans absorbed heavy casualties, but they eventually got control of the airport west of Khania and were able to land reinforcements. All organized resistance ended on May 30, and the British troops fled across to the southern coast of the island, where most of them were taken off to **Egypt.**

Some did not get away, however. Not only were many killed, but some were stranded in the mountains. At great risk to their own lives and their families and communities, many Cretans hid these troops until they could be taken off. Meanwhile, the British sent in special agents who-disguised as Cretans - helped to coordinate the resistance by the Cretans. Based in the mountains, these Cretan resistance fighters continued to harrass the **German occupation forces;** the most famous incident involved the kidnapping of the German Commandant and, after leading him for many days across the Cretan mountains, removing him on an English boat. But Cretans paid dearly for these acts of defiance: several villages were destroyed, their male inhabitants killed, and there were hard times for most Cretans.

When the last German troops surrendered in May 1945, Crete started on the road to recovery. Several cities such as Iraklion and Khania had suffered extensive damage from air raids, commerce and transport was all but non-

Morosini Fountain (1626) Iraklion

existent, and agriculture was barely beyond the survival stage. The United Nations aided Crete in the first months, but soon the Cretans were moving on their own. The civil war that so divided other parts of Greece at least did not split Crete. As the economy revived, increasing numbers of tourists began to arrive each year-some drawn by the archaeological remains, others by the natural pleasures. In the 1.960s, touristic development on the grand scale occurred, and Crete entered into a new phase of expansion and change. Not everyone likes everything that has happened as a result, but all must agree that the island is a more dynamic place than ever before.

2. Visiting Crete

It is possible to spend only a few hours on Crete-as thousands of tourists do when they come with a cruise ship-and leave feeling you have experienced something special. And there are people who have spent twenty years on Crete and still feel they don't know enough about the island. It is that kind of a place. Between these two extremes is where most visitors come, and with a little planning quite a lot of Crete can be seen in relatively few days. Much depends on the form of transportation used. With your own car (or motorbike) you can cover a great deal of Crete in 4-5 days. Public buses require considerable planning to take best advantage of the schedules. Others may prefer taxis-or hitchhiking.

And because of individual differences as to what are the goals of traveling on Crete, it is impossible to set out an itinerary suitable to everyone. That said, here is a suggested 5-day itinerary for Crete to give some idea of what's possible.

Day 1: **Iraklion**, including the **Archaeological Museum** - the **Palace of Knossos.** Those who like to move might wind up the day with a visit to **Arkhanes** (for archaeology), **Fodhele** (for El Greco), the **Cave of Eileithyia** (for mythology), or just a nearby beach.

Day 2: To **Ayios Nikolaos,** with a brief stop at **Mallia**-eastward with stop at **Gournia**-down to **Kato Zakros** (for archaeology) or on to **Vai** (for tropical beach)-overnight in **Sitia** or back in **Ayios Nikolaos.**

Day 3: Down to **Phaestos**-stop at **Gortyna**-possibly **Ayia Triadha** (for archaeology)-down to **Matala** for beach and caves-perhaps on to **Ayia Galini** for overnight.

Day 4: To **Rethymnon**-sidetrip to **Monastery** of **Arkadhi** (and possibly to **Margarites** for pottery or **Melidhoni** for cave-on to **Khania** for overnight.

Day 5: Either: Walking around **Khania**, up to **Akrotiri**, possibly excursion to west (**Kastelli** or **Phalasarna**)

Or: Long-day's excursion through **Gorge** of **Samaria** (depending on season).
Now you're on your own!

CENTRAL CRETE
IRAKLION

Most visitors to Crete spend some time in **Iraklion,** Crete's largest city (about 85,000) and its administrative capital. There is no denying that it has become so developed, so crowded, so modern, that its more indigenous and picturesque aspects are no longer much in evidence. But Iraklion is a necessary crossroads for tourism-with its airline, ship, and bus terminals, its many hotels, its travel agents, gift-shops, etc.-and also for those more interested in archaeology-both as the gateway to **Knossos** and for its great museum collection. And Iraklion still has more historical, archaeological, and other points of interest than is generally realized, and can well repay anyone willing to leave the main streets and wander about seeking either specific landmarks or just random sights.

The major historical imprint on Iraklion was left by the Venetians during their four and one half centuries of rule in this, their capital city, known as **Candia.** If Iraklion had been settled in Minoan times, no traces have been found except for tombs on the edge of the modern city. Little of the centuries of Byzantine Crete survived, either. It was the Venetians who built the great walls, the striking fort on the harbor, the various churches, and the two showpieces of the city-the **Morosini Fountain** and the **Loggia.** Two centuries of Turkish rule left little except some fountains and private houses. As a result, when Iraklion came to be renovated in the decades following **World War II,** not that much of the old city was taken down. What the city lost, rather, was more what might be called a vaguely Middle Eastern bazaar atmosphere.

But something of the old buildings and old atmosphere

Elounda Beach

does remain, and the best way to appreciate this is to take a walking tour around the city, before or after you have paid homage to the Minoans. You could plunge in almost anywhere, but many people head first for the office of the **National Tourist Organization,** opposite the **Archaeological Museum,** to get information about the island's tourist accommodations, travel facilities, sites, etc. As you leave that office, turn right and proceed into the **Plateia Eleftheria,** or **Liberty Square,** a favorite gathering place for natives and foreigners, with its many cafes and restaurants spilling over into every available street and traffic island. Try a meal here-and watch your waiter dodge the traffic with his tray of meals-or come by in the evening and have an ice cream or coffee and watch all of Iraklion parade by on the **volta,** or evening stroll.

There was once an aqueduct in this square and a great gate in the **Venetian walls** that led down an inclined ramp to the coast road, but these were long ago demolished. Now there are several monuments around the square: the central statue is in honor of the **unknown soldiers of Crete**; on a terrace on the Venetian wall is a statue of **Eleftherios Venizelos, Crete's** gift to 20th-century political life (p. 24); and on one of the small islands is a bust of **Kazantzakis,** another Cretan and one of Greece's best-known modern authors. Often there is an amusement park operating along one side of the square, and extending behind that is the city's garden-park, a refreshing oasis.

With the statue to the unknown soldier behind you, head down Iraklion's main shopping street, **Dikeosinis,** its right side lined with shops and its left side with public buildings. A short distance down on the left is a small clearing with a bust of **Daskaloyiannis** (see p. 23) and steps leading to the square also named after him. The **Post Office** is located at the far end of that square. Continuing along Dikeosinis Street, you pass the **Tourist Police office** just before **Evans Street** (named after the excavator of Knossos) and the next street to the left, officially named 1866 Street but obviously **Market Street.**

Even if you can think of nothing you want to purchase,

Venetian Loggia (16C) Iraklion

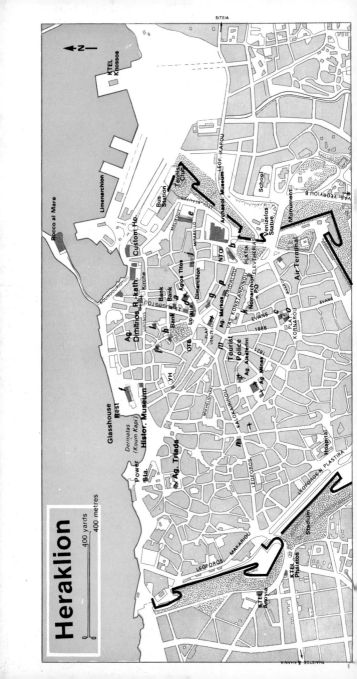

you should walk up Market Street: you'll want something before you're through. The produce overflows onto the street-every possible kind of vegetables and fruits, and many other Cretan products. Boisterous, chaotic, jampacked, it's a reminder that not all the old ways have been overwhelmed. And about 50 meters up, on the left, is a short narrow alley, often crammed with people eating at the tables set out by the little restaurants on both sides. Known as **"Dirty Alley"** (from the old locals who used to eat here), it is now a place where every foreigner has at least one meal.

Proceeding down Market Street to the end, you come to **Kornarou Square,** with its hexagonal **Turkish fountain** (now restored and housing a gift shop) and the **Bembo Fountain,** named after the Venetian who built it in 1588, incorporating a headless **Roman statue** found elsewhere on Crete. Leaving Kornarou Square by the main street off to the right - **Vikela** - you come after about three blocks to the square before Iraklion's modern **Cathedral.** Begun in 1862 and not formally inaugurated until 1895, it is one of the largest Orthodox churches in Greece. Its interior is painted with frescoes that will strike most foreigners as needing some "aging". The church is dedicated to **Ayios Menas,** Iraklion's patron saint, who also gave his name to the small church on the level below, and to the left of, the front of the cathedral. This church, which dates to at least the early 18th century, has several ikons and

A Lion from Morosini Fountain

an ikonostasis (or chancel screen) worthy of inspecting.

Staying on that lower level and moving across the lower square toward the rear of the cathedral, you come to two old churches. The one to the left is **Ayii Dheka** ("the holy ten," after **10 Cretans** killed by Romans in the 3rd century), dating from the 17th century. To the right of this is **Ayia Katerina,** named after the same Saint Catherine who is honored by the great Orthodox monastery on **Mt. Sinai.** This order of monks established a school here about 1550, and although there is actually little evidence for it, claims are made that many notable Cretans, including El Greco, studied here. Now the interior of the church has been cleared and it is a **museum of Cretan - Byzantine art** and ecclesiastical objects. Its most notable exhibits are six ikons by **Michael Damaskinos;** a slightly older contemporary of El Greco, he also went to Venice, but Damaskinos returned to Crete and painted these works here. Even those not especially knowledgable about painting might enjoy seeing the fusion of the Byzantine and Italian-Renaissance styles. (The museum keeps fairly regular hours and charges a slight fee; No photographs are allowed).

Standing in the lower square, and with the side of the Cathedral to your back, head through one of the narrow streets that lead out into

Venetian fortress (1523-40) Iraklion   *Outside a Coffee shop*

Kalakairinou Street, what might be called the average **Iraklionot's shopping street,** and all that more interesting for having relatively few shops aimed at tourists. Turn left and proceed some ten blocks until you come to the square before the so-called **Khania Gate.** A handsome gate built by the Venetians about 1570, and traditionally known as the **Gate** of the **Pantokrator** or **Panigra gate,** its broad archway is a modern opening to accommodate traffic; if you've come this far, look into the original passageway to the right. And just outside stands the imposing bronze statue of **Captain Mikhalis Korakas,** one of the heroes of Crete's 19th-century struggles against the Turks. This is the gateway to **Khania** and the west and also to **Phaestos** and the south.

Now reverse your route along Kalokairinou, staying on the left (or north) side for about six blocks until you come to the street named after **Stylianos Giamalakis,** a surgeon who assembled the collection of antiquities that now occupies a special room in the **Archaeological Museum** (p. 31). Turning left here, you proceed down Giamalakis Street, passing on the right (third street), **Kazantzakis Street,** named for the writer who was born on this street. (The original house is gone, but there is a plaque at No. 18 to indicate the site.) When you come out at the end of Giamalakis Street, you face the sea.

Turn right and follow the sea road and you come at once to the **Xenia Hotel,** on the left, and just opposite, The **Historical** and **Ethnographic Museum.** (It observes normal hours and charges a modest fee). This is housed in the former mansion of a prominent **Cretan family, Kalakairinou,** with a modern addition. It takes up with the Roman period on Crete, and continues through the Byzantine, Venetian, Turkish, and modern periods, and is well worth even a brief visit. There are some remains of the early **Christian churches** of Crete; some fine architectural elements from the Venetian period, including some quite elegant stone carvings; some Turkish inscriptions, **tombstones,** and **carvings;** some frescoes removed from medieval chapels as well as some **Byzantine ikons;** mementoes of Crete's struggles against the Turks; two "re-created" studies, one of **Kazantzakis,** and the other of **Emmanuel Tsouderos,** a Cretan and Premier of Greece when the Germans invaded in 1941; and on the uppermost floor, some superb examples of Cretan popular

arts and crafts-particularly textiles and domestic wares of all sorts.

Proceeding along the coast road, you come up to the harbor mole that leads out to the great **Venetian fort.** Everyone should at least go out and examine the exterior and see the **Lion of St. Mark,** confirmation of the Venetian presence here. Those with a little extra time might want to inspect the interior. (Regular hours, modest fee). Although there had been previous forts on this site, this one dates from the early 16th century; in the 1960s-70s, it was given a major restoration, with the result that it is now one of the most impressive Italian-Renaissance forts you will see anyplace in Europe. You can walk about and peer through the great thick walls and go up onto the battlements and imagine what it must have been like to hold off the great siege of the Turks.

From the fort, too, you get a good view of the remains of the Venetian **arsenali** along the shore side of the old harbor. These arsenals were more what we would call shipyards, for here is where the Venetians repaired and restocked their ships that plied the Mediterranean to promote their commercial empire. When you leave the fort, you may want to step over and take a closer look at these (now restored) arsenals-but realize that the water once came right up to them. But then, with your back to the harbor (and the mole to the fort), you will now head up the steep **"25th of August Street,"** long the most familiar street to everyone who visited Crete, for almost everyone entered by ship at the port of Iraklion. To this day, it is lined with most of the major tourist agencies, ticket agents, car rentals, and a fair share of tourist souvenir shops.

Proceeding up the street, you come on your left to the

Bembo fountain (1588) Iraclion

square in front of **St. Titus,** dedicated to the early leader of the Christian community on Crete, the recipient of one of the **Apostle Paul's epistles,** and now the patron saint of the island. This structure has gone through several major reconstructions since the 15th century, and for long served as a Turkish mosque.

If hardly notable as church architecture, both the interior and exterior reward a walk-around. Inside, too, is one of the most revered treasures of Christian Crete, the skull of **St. Titus,** which the Venetians carried off in the 17th century and only returned to the Cretans. in 1966.

Just up **25th of August Street** is the **Venetian Loggia,** a building that served the leaders of the Venetian community as a sort of "gentlemen's club". The original was erected in the 1620s and combined a mixture of **Italian-Renaissance** elements. Over the centuries it fell into disrepair and earthquakes took their toll; by the time it was decided to reconstruct it, only fragments of the original survived, so what you see today is essentially a completely new **Loggia** but built to the original plans and incorporating every possible architectural detail. It is one of several surprises on Crete.

Built into the lower left side, by the way, is what remains of the **Sagredo Fountain,** another Venetian work, from about 1603; the relief carving of a woman is believed to represent Crete. And directly abutting the rear of the Loggia is another Venetian structure, the **Armeria,** or armory, which now serves as **Iraklion's City Hall.** Proceeding up **25th of August Street** you come into

Kallergon Square. Off to the right is the entrance into **El Greco Park,** another pleasant resting place (and with public toilets); the **Telephone** and **Telegraph office** is along the far side of this.

Proceeding straight ahead out of **Kallergon Square,** you pass on your left the **Church of St. Mark's.** Considerably restored and rebuilt, this was probably the first **Venetian church** in their new city of Candia, and it was fittingly dedicated to their own patron saint. (It once had its campanile, or bell-tower.) The Turks converted it into a mosque, and today it serves as a hall for art exhibitions and concerts or meetings. Around its walls is a permanent exhibit of reproductions of some of the notable Byzantine frescoes in Crete's churches.

St. Mark's looked out on the main square of Venetian Crete, and the centerpiece of that square then-and in some ways to this day-is the fountain that was constructed in 1627-28. Since it was commissioned by the then Governor General of Candia, as Crete was known by the Venetians, **Francesco Morosini,** the fountain and square are sometimes still called by this name, Morosini. (He also commissioned the Loggia-but it was his nephew who later directed the defense against the siege of the Turks). Originally there was a statue of **Neptune,** or **Poseidon** atop the fountain; the four lions are possibly from some previous work; but the eight elegant bays, or lobes, with their now fading relief carvings remind us of the era when Iraklion was a satellite of the Italian Renaissance.

For some, this may be a

fitting place to end a tour of the city and sit down and enjoy a refreshment. There are many other points of interest, of course-numerous churches and fountains, many interesting old houses. Then there are the Venetian walls; cleared of the dirt and vegetation and shacks that had long covered many sections, they now offer a dramatic impression of 16th-century Italian fortifications. And on one of the bastions, **Martinengo,** to the southwest, is the tomb of **Kazantzakis,** which many people visit to pay tribute to this exemplar of what he called "**the Cretan glance**", that special Cretan spirit. From this bastion, too, you enjoy a good view of **Mt. Iouktas,** which appears like a giant recumbent head and so was considered by the ancients to be the burial place of **Zeus.**

But for those who have not yet visited it, the **Archaeological Museum** remains as the major attraction of Iraklion. You can make your way there by leaving **Fountain Square** by **Daedalou Street,** the pedestrian mall that goes off the west side. Lined with tavernas and gift shops, **Daedalou** leads onto the corner of **Liberty Square,** and you proceed on along the edge to the **Archaeological Museum.**

THE
ARCHAEOLOGICAL
MUSEUM

This is the world's leading collection of **Minoan** art and culture and is clearly one of the major attractions of Crete. The hours and days of closing tend to change from year to year, but it is usually open for regular hours. Some people stroll through it and see the highlights in an hour or less. Others can pass hours and return over and over again. The displays are well laid out; the general sequence of rooms is chronological, but within that frame individual rooms concentrate on specific sites or areas. Most of the exhibits are labeled in Greek, English, and French, so you can usually know at least the basic identification of what you are looking at.

You proceed into **Room I,** with its remains from the **Neolithic** and **Pre-Palatial Minoan culture** (6000-2000 B.C.). Many of the neolithic remains are from caves, while the prepalatial finds are from vaulted tombs. Already several of the familiar motifs and works of the **Minoan culture** are evident-the fine carved sealstones, for instance, or the three men in the horns of a bull (Case 12).

Inside a Coffee shop in Kastelli, Iraklion

Rooms II and **III** are finds from the **Proto-Palatial Period** (2000-1700 B.C.), the time when the first great great palaces were erected at **Knossos, Phaestos**, and **Mallia**. You will hardly need to be asked to admire some of the lovely **Kamares-style** pottery. In Case 26 is the **Town Mosaic;** made of faience (painted earthenware) it has played a crucial role in allowing archaeologists to see what Minoan structures actually looked like. And in Case 41 is the famed **Phaestos Disc:** 45 different characters were first carved and then punched into the soft clay-perhaps the first instance of movable type! It is assumed that each character represents an idea or a syllable and that they should be read by spiraling from the circumference to the center. But beyond that, the experts cannot agree, either as to what language it records or what the text is.

Room IV begins a series of rooms with finds from the **Neo-Palatial period** (1700-1400 B.C.), the time when the new and grander palaces were erected and **Minoan civilization**

Iraklion Market

burst into full bloom. There is no end to the treasures and delights: The **Snake Goddesses** (Case 50); the gold-and-ivory acrobat (Case 56); the **Royal Gameboard** (Case 57); **Linear A** and **Linear B** tablets (Case 69); the model of a two-story house (Case 70A); an ivory cosmetic box (Case 79A); the **Harvester Vase** (Case 94) and **Athletes' Rhyton** (Case 96); the celebrated bee pendant (Case 101); the libation vase with the sanctuary and a leaping wild goat (Case 111); bronze tools and weapons (Case 127); a superb selection of sealstones (Case 128).

When you enter **Room X** you are seeing the **Post-Palatial** culture from the time (1400-1100 B.C.) when the **Mycenaeans** seem to have been in command at least of **Knossos** and the major palaces. You will want to note the ceramic group of dancers around a lyre-player (Case 132) and the crater with a warrior on horseback (Case 141), the first such representation known from Crete.

Rooms XI and **XII** display finds from the **Sub-Minoan** and **Geometric periods** (1100-750 B.C.), by which time the pure **Minoan civilization** was fading and the **Dorian-Greek** culture was introducing new elements. There are the first iron weapons and tools known from Crete (Case 153), and the earliest known transparent glass from Crete (Case 162). Note, too, a more recognizably human touch in the painting of the loving couple on a jug (Case 163).

Room XIII has a large selection of the **two types of**

sarcophagi used by the later Minoans-the bathtub shape and the rectangular -chest type. The dead person's legs were folded against the upper body (see remains of a burial in the corner). Also hardly to be missed in this room is a large wooden model of the Palace of Knossos.

Proceeding upstairs, you will come into a large hall with its dazzling display of Minoan frescoes, dated from about 1600 to 1400 B.C. The original fragments remain clearly distinguishable from the reconstructed sections (most of which were done by two Swiss artists working under **Sir Arthur Evans,** the **Gilliérons,** father and son). The fresco depicting the bull-leapers will perhaps seem the most dramatic, but many others repay examination. And in the center of the room is one of the most valuable of all Minoan remains, the painted sarcophagus found in a tomb near the **Ayia Triadha** site. Dated to about 1400 B.C., it provides a unique view of Minoan religious rites, presumably the burial service for the notable who was in this sarcophagus. And in two small adjacent **rooms, XV** and **XVI** there are more frescoes, including the often-reproduced **"Parisienne",** or head of an elegant young lady (in fact, probably a priestess). Note, too, the **"Captain of the Blacks",** the latter possibly a troop of mercenaries from **Africa.**

Room XVII is given over to the collection of **Stylianos Giamalakis,** the prominent Cretan surgeon who was allowed by the Greek government to buy Minoan antiquities (it is claimed, so that

A Closer View of the Venetian Fort: Iraklion

Cretans who found any would feel they were circumventing the government!). Among its prize Minoan pieces is the gold diadem (Case 191); of the later works, there is the handsome bronze statuette of a man carrying a ram (Case 178), dated to about 750 B.C.

The remaining **rooms-XVIII,** upstairs, and **XIX** and **XX,** downstairs (and now often closed to the public)-display works from **Archaic** (750-480 BC) **Classical** (480-325 B.C.), **Hellenistic** and **Roman** (325 BC-AD 400) from various sites around Crete. Many of the objects are of considerable importance to students of art and architecture as they reveal Crete's role in developing new forms and methods in the **Archaic Period,** but even to the amateur they provide a sense of the continuity of culture on Crete during those many centuries.

KNOSSOS

Surely one of the great archaeological sites of the entire world, the **Palace of Knossos** is a "must" for almost everyone who comes to Crete. 39

Even if you are not that interested in "old ruins" or the details of Minoan civilization, **Knossos** makes an irresistible impact by its sheer size and complexity. It both memorializes and creates Minoan civilization for the modern sensibility.

It is open to the public virtually every day of the year (major holidays excepted), and generally from early morning till sundown. The admission fee, whatever it is at the moment, is worth it. And there is no fee for taking pictures with hand-held cameras. Since it is only about 5 km. from Iraklion, you could consider walking at least one way, although the road is now heavily traveled. There are frequent public buses to and from the site. There are always taxis or rented motorbikes. Since almost a half million visitors go through Knossos each year now, it can get very crowded and even noisy during the peak hours of the peak tourist season. If you have the choice, get out very early in the day. But whenever or however, go.

Most people are not prepared for the extend and state of the remains of the palace, and you could emerge from a long tour of the site quite baffled if you knew nothing about how it came to be in this condition. Although there must have been considerable destruction by even, say, 1100 BC, it is unlikely that such a mammoth structure just vanished overnight. Probably it was abandoned in bits and pieces, as floors and walls collapsed; slowly the earth blew over it and vegetation took hold. By the time the Romans appeared (say, 65 BC), there must have been a fair amount of the Minoan structure still above the surface; a thousand years later, however, it is fair to say that most of it was buried. Yet references by medieval and Renaissance historians and scholars and travelers make it clear that Knossos was known to have been there.

But it was not until 1878 that a local antiquarian, **Minos Kalokairinos,** made a trial dig on the site. He actually turned up some large urns as well as walls and rooms, but the Turkish authorities made him stop. The great **Schliemann,** however, heard of these finds and came over to Crete in 1883 intending to extend his series of spectacular discoveries. When he could not agree on terms with the owner of the land, Schliemann left. And so it was left to **Arthur Evans,** an Oxford scholar whose interest in the inscriptions on sealstones from Crete first brought him over to the island in 1894. On his trip around the island, he soon realized that it was filled with archaeological remains, and he became determined to acquire the site of Knossos. Not until after the Turks were forced out in 1898, though, could he get official permission. And it was March, 1900, before he and his crew put the first spade into the

Sarcophagos: Iraklion Museum

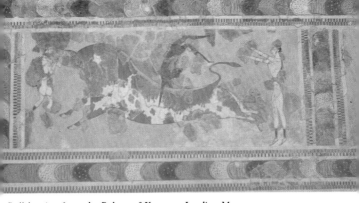

Bull-leaping from the Palace of Knossos: Iraclion Museum

earth above the palace.

Almost from the first, **Evans** was rewarded with plentiful and provocative finds. Within the first three years, the major portions of the palace had been revealed. Evans continued to direct the excavations into the 1930s, spending a large part of his personal fortune on this and the many other sites he discovered around Crete. The **British School of Archaeology,** however, took over formal responsibility for the site, and in 1952 they turned it over to the Greek archaeological authorities. The British have maintained their strong links with Knossos, however, and continue to excavate here.

Almost from the first, Evans had confronted a problem. Here was this vast, multi-storied palace that had pretty much collapsed down onto itself. And although many of the elements had disappeared-all the wood, for instance-and much was beyond use, there was a great deal of the original left: stairs, walls, floors, corridors, supporting posts, and much more. So Evans chose to reconstruct as much of the palace as he could, using reinforced concrete for the missing elements, but incorporating as much of the original as possible. He "color coded" his reconstructed elements-yellow, for instance,, being wooden framework, red the inverted trees for columns. And he often had to make some speculative reconstuctions where there just wasn't that much of the original left. The many frescoes presented a special challenge; he commissioned artists (see p. 39) to finish the paintings after he and his staff had assembled the original fragments; these works were removed to the museum and complete replicas were made and placed around the palace.

Not all the experts appreciate all the reconstructing that Evans did at Knossos. But for most people, this is what makes this palace so unforgettable. So convincing is the reconstruction, in fact, so thoroughly evocative of a way of life, that many visitors might need reminding: this is not the way the mass of Minoans lived. This was the residence and capital and administrative headquarters for those at the apex of 41

Throne Room: Knossos

TOURING THE PALACE

Everyone must enter the palace at its **West Court** with its raised causeways. To the left are three round, deep walled pits; as they seem not to have been plastered, they could not have served as cisterns so they may have been storage, silos for grain; eventually they were used as refuse pits. Most people enter the palace by turning right along this facade, but this is not necessary (and you may avoid some crowds) if you turn to the left and go straight over to the so-called **Theatral Area.** These are actually two tiers of steps at right angles, and although there was mostly nothing like what we consider a play or theater to be viewed here, it is not unlikely that ceremonial processions or other rites were witnessed from these steps. Because if you stand on the steps you can look down the extraordinary **Royal Road,** now exposed for a distance of some 150 yards (but originally connecting to the **Little Palace** on a nearby slope). It was lined with houses and workshops but strikes us today as far too impressive to have been used for everyday traffic.

Leaving the **Theatral Area** at your back, you walk towards the north side of the palace. Immediately to the left is a freestanding chamber, the **North Lustral Basin.** Evans found many such rooms in the palace, and deduced from several elements that they must have been used to hold water; he also decided that they were used for more than just routine bathing; thus his word "lustral" to reflect the religious-ritual nature of the cleansing process. Leaving

Minoan society. And whether the ruling family also functioned as the top religious hierarchy or not, the palace of Knossos must have served as the chief religious force. Everything, indeed, must have been interrelated for the Minoans: the control of the island's economy, its agricultural produce, taxes or tribute, the administrative bureaucracy, rituals and festivities-all were related and all came to focus on Knossos and the other major palaces.

So you are not seeing how the masses lived-almost all of whom must have tended fields or animals-but you are seeing much more than what we today understand by the word "palace". And if Evans went a bit too far in assigning names and functions to the many rooms, the fact is that the rooms are there, just as the finds are in the museum. Don't worry about the scholars' quarrels over dates and specifics. Just walk through the palace and let it works its spell on you.

that behind you and proceeding further east, you enter through a gateway into the **North Pillar Hall;** the bases of the pillars and columns indicate there was originally a second story above, but the exact function of this hall is not known.

You turn to the right and proceed up an inclined ramp, the **North Entrance Passage.** Originally much wider-for many elements of the first palace were modified when incorporated into the second palace-it was flanked by two-storied bastions; the one on the west side has been reconstructed, and about half-way up the ramp you can take the stairway on the right to the upper story and examine the relief-fresco of the bull (exactly where the original was found). Proceeding up the entrance ramp, you climb a few stairs and find yourself looking onto the great **Central Court.** Some 53 m. by 27 m., this court was paved with flagstones of which only a few have survived. And if it seems highly unlikely that

bulls were running around this courtyard in the bull-leaping ceremony, it must have seen its share of other Minoan ceremonies. Realize, however, that it was enclosed by two-and three-story buildings-that the Minoans did not enjoy the natural and open panorama we now appreciate.

Off to the right side as you come onto the court, notice the subterranean drainage pipe left exposed - some of the still-functioning plumbing that the Minoans enjoyed. But now head diagonally across the north end of the court to the little (modern) flight of stairs that bring you down to a lower story. Off to the right is the **Corridor of the Bays,** a storeroom; adjacent to that is the **Magazine of the Medallion Pithoi**-"magazine" in this usage being a storeroom (as in "powder magazine") and the **pithoi** being the giant urns; and then adjacent to the latter is the **Room of the Stone Drain,** so named from the large stone and channel that drain down onto the lower **Court of the**

Knossos

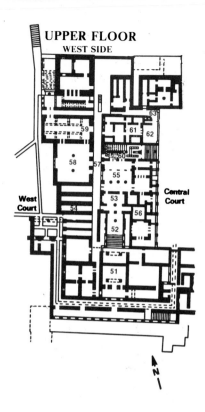

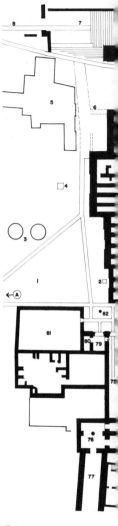

UPPER FLOOR
WEST SIDE

West Court

Central Court

A To Entry Pavillion
1. West Court
2. Altar
3. Walled Pits
4. Altar
5. Northwest Treasure House
6. Incised Stone
7. Theatral Area
8. Royal Road
9. North Lustral Basin
10. Northwest Portico

11. Outer Gate
B To Pillar Crypt
12. North Pillar Hall
13. North Entrance Passage
14. Bull Fresco-Relief
15. Central Court
16. Pits and Shrine
17. Stairs (To East Quarter)
18. Corridor of the Bays
19. Magazine of the Medallion Pithoi
20. Room of the Stone Drain

THE PALACE OF KNOSSOS

MAIN AREAS

1. Corridor of the Draughtboard
2. Royal Pottery Stores
3. Magazines of the Giant Pithoi
4. East Bastion
5. Court of the Stone Spout
6. Potters' Workshop
7. Lapidaries' Workshop
8. Lower East - West Corridor
9. King's Megaron (or Hall of the Double Axes)
10. Portico

31. Queen's Megaron
32. Queen's Dressing Room
33. Court of the Distaffs
34. Treasury
35. Gallery and Lightwell (Hall of Colonnades)
36. Grand Staircase
37. Bathroom
38. Room with 3 Urns
39. Shrine of the Double Axes
40. Corridor of the Sword-Tablets

Stone Spout. Leaving this Room to your rear, you walk north a bit along the **Corridor of the Draughtboard** (so named because it was here that was found the gameboard now in Case 57 in the **Archaeological Museum**)-"draughts" being the British term for the game of checkers.

From this corridor, you turn right and descend a fairly narrow flight of stairs, passing on your left the **Magazine of the Giant Pithoi:** they hardly require any description. At the bottom of the stairs you come to a now closed gate but you can peer over and get some impression of the **East Bastion** -an entryway with an ingenious system of conduits running down along the side of the stairs to control the flow of water. Returning up the stairs as far as the **Magazine of the Giant Pithoi,** you turn left there and step into the **Court of the Stone Spout.** Proceeding straight on (southward), you pass through the **Potters Workshop**-with its benches and receptacles (for holding clay). Still moving straight on, note on the left the **Lapidaries Worshop** with its chunks of

greenish basalt (imported from **Sparta!**). Moving along this narrow corridor, you turn right into an enclosed corridor and proceed about 20 feet before turning left into the **King's Megaron**-this last word being the Greek for "large room", in sense of "main hall". To the left (east), through a series of doorways, is the **Portico** (where a wooden replica of the famous throne sits); this **Portico** is bordered on two sides by a colonnade. On the right side of the **King's Megaron,** behind a pair of columns, is a light well, on the wall of which you should be able to make out inscribed signs of the double axe so associated with Minoan ritual life.

You leave the King's Megaron by the doorway directly opposite that by which you entered; following the passageway, you come into the **Queen's Megaron,** with its more gentle proportions and elements and the replica of the dolphin fresco suggesting that Evans was right to assign this to the Queen. On one side (right as you enter) is a small chamber that was quite likely

46

he bathroom. But proceeding off the corridor to the right, you turn and come into the Queen's Dressing Room. Just to the right as you enter is the remains of what has been called the "flush toilet": whether there was actually running water to carry off the waste is uncertain, but it does seem to have been a toilet.

Leave this dressing room by the corridor that passes over the drainage system and wind

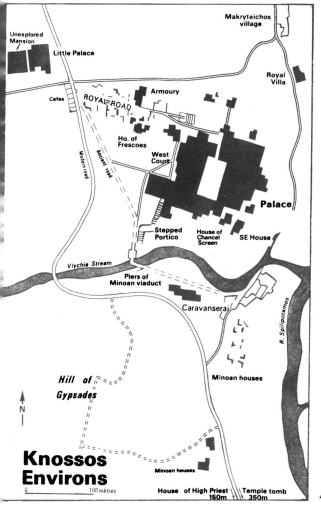

Knossos
Environs

0 ___ 100 mètres

around until you come out onto the open gallery, or Hall of the Colonnades. (The King's Megaron is to the right, the lightwell of the **Grand Staircase** to the left). Ascend the Grand Staircase, notice how much wear-and-tear the relatively soft gypsum steps are taking-more from the millions of hard-soled tourists, probably, than from the soft-soled Minoans. Everyone should walk to the very top of the Grand Staircase, just to get the full sensation, and once there you have a choice. Some might want to go halfway back down the stairs to the first landing, the **Upper Hall of the Colonnades,** with its replicas of the great figure-of-eight shields. Then, leaving this area (with the shields on your right), you could walk on and explore the whole southeastern corner of the palace-and come back up onto the **Central Court** by a dirt ramp at its southeast corner.

But most of the remains in that area hold little interest for the general visitor, so you are to emerge onto the Central Court **at the top of the Grand Staircase** and cut diagonally down to the south edge of the Court and the **Corridor of the Priest King,** with its fresco of the so-called **Prince with the Lily Crown.** Leaving this behind you, make your way to the south edge of the palace and the sacral horns-placed there by Evans, but known from other evidence to have been used as a decorative element around the palace. This is a good place to get oriented. You are looking south here, with **Mt. Iouktas,** or the head of the dead Zeus (see p. 37) in the distance. In the immediate foreground is

the hill of **Gypsadhes,** where much of the gypsum used in constructing the palace was quarried. Down the slopes below the palace was a viaduct that connected the **Stepped Portico** and **South House** (the structures at the southwest corner below the palace) with the **Caravanserai,** a sort of reception inn for "caravans", (which can be visited on an opposite slope only by leaving the palace and following the modern road around the bend to come in from above it).

You now turn to your right and proceed over to the **South** (or **Great) Propylaeum,** the entryway recognizable from the replica of one of the **Cup-bearers,** which formed a long fresco on the **Corridor of the Procession.** You turn right (north) and climb the **Great Staircase** to come up onto what Evans called the **"Piano Nobile"**-Italian for "noble floor". You will want to do two things from up here. One is to look down (to your left) onto the impressive **West Magazines,** with their many bays, storage urns, and several (visible) cists, or subterranean storage pits. And then you proceed straight on until you come opposite an enclosed room to your right; make your way into that to see some of the replicas of the smaller frescoes, and then step out onto the small terrace that overlooks the **Central Court.** Leaving this terrace by a tiny flight of stairs (to the left), you come down onto the edge of the **Central Court** but immediately turn right and descend the few stairs into the **Anteroom of the Throne Room,** the fitting climax to a visit to this palace.

In the center is a bowl of

porphyry, which Evans actually found nearby but placed here because he felt it might have been used for some purification ritual before entering the **Throne Room** proper. Until the early 1970s, every visitor to Knossos could enter that room and sit on the actual throne, dating from at least 1400 B.C. and certainly the oldest throne in Europe. Now you must content yourself with looking at it and the benches against the walls. (This throne was copied for the chair of the presiding judge of the **Court of International Justice** at the **Hague**.) The frescoes of the wingless griffins employ a traditional symbol of the power of gods and kings (and the griffin is Iraklion's modern symbol). The sunken room to the left is another **Lustral Chamber**.

Stepping out onto the **Central Court,** you now proceed (south) along its side, passing various elements such as the stairs that once led up to the top of the palace; the **Tripartite** (or **Columnar**) **Shrine,** with the **Lobby** of the Stone Seat **and the** Temple Repositories (off to the rear); and the **Pillar Crypts**—two rooms (now off-limits) which have double-ax signs carved into their supporting pillars, indicating these rooms served some role in an important religious cult of the Minoans. Moving out of the south side of the Lobby of the Stone Seat, you step across an area where Evans found a building that has been variously indentified as a Mycenaean megaron or a later Greek temple. Cut over to the **South Propylaeum,** to the right), and then leave that through a restored doorway; turn right and then left, and then come out onto the flagstones of the **Corridor of the Procession,** and originally lined with walls painted with the procession of gift-bearers. Turn right onto this corridor and you come out onto the **West Court,** your tour through the palace completed.

For those interested, of course, there could be many more elements to pursue. In the immediate environs of the main palace, for instance, there are several dependencies: the **Caravanserai** and **Viaduct** have already been mentioned (p. 48) as has the **Little Palace** (which was linked by the Royal Road, p. 42). Adjacent to the **Little Palace** is the so-called **Unexplored Mansion** and a newly discovered **Roman House.** Beyond the Caravanserai, off the same modern road, is the **Royal Temple Tomb.** And down along the banks of the tiny **Kairatos River** to the north of the palace is the **Royal Villa.** If you had a desire to investigate any of these, you should make arrangements at the **Archaeological Museum** beforehand. Of perhaps more interest is the **Roman villa of Dionysus,** which can be visited at any time; it sits some 500 yards north of the palace, just off the main road from Iraklion (to the left as you head back toward Iraklion): the red-tiled roof of the modern shelter is what you head for. The villa received its name from the motif of the mosaic still to be seen, and although there is nothing spectacular about the remains, they provide an unexpected dimension to the long story of life at Knossos.

EXCURSIONS FROM IRAKLION

There are numerous excursions - of varying ambition and duration and with a variety of destinations-that you can take from Iraklion. Indeed, Iraklion could be used as a "homebase" from which to visit virtually all of the island, but this would require a lot of travelling back each night. Here are described all the more important excursions that can reasonably done in a one-day roundtrip (for each) from Iraklion.

THE PLAIN OF THE WINDMILLS & THE BIRTHPLACE OF ZEUS

This is a full day's excursion to two of Crete's best-known natural landmarks: **Lasithi Plain,** with its thousands of windmills, and the **Dhiktaion Cave,** claimed as the **mythical birthplace of Zeus**. The ride

Magazines of Giant Pithoi

there and the view of the plain will reward those who just like to look; the descent into the cave (which sits above one edge of the plain) will provide a climax for those who are more active.

You leave Iraklion by the main route to the east, taking either the old coast road after the airport or staying on the new national highway. In either case, the two merge at about the 17 km. point, and at the 22 km. point you observe the sign indicating a turn off to the right to **Lasithi.** Soon you are climbing the **Dhikti,** or **Lasithi, Mountains,** passing through **Potamies** (with its **Church of Christos** with Byzantine frescoes) and **Avdou** (with its **Church of Ayios Antonios,** also with Byzantine frescoes). At 46 km. you come to a turnoff into the village of **Krasi**-well worth taking to see the gigantic plane tree and its adjacent spring. Proceeding along the main road, you pass (at 49 km.) the **Monastery of Panayia Kera,** with important frescoes, discovered under paint only in the early 1960s.

As you come along a winding, climbing pass, at about 52 km. you see a line of old stone windmills along the ridge, and then, suddenly spread out below you is the **Lasithi Plain.** About 9 km. long and 4-7 km. wide, it appears like a vast stadium ringed by the mountains. It has long been cultivated-Minoan remains have been found on many of the surrounding slopes-and is still one of the more productive areas of Crete. Part of this fertility is due to the fact that the rain water drains down from the slopes and seeps into the limestone below the soil, and although much of that water then drains away, much remains to be tapped. And that is what the windmills do: pump up the water to irrigate the fields. In recent years many of them have been allowed to sit idle as the farmers shifted to gasoline-powered pumps, but the price of gasoline may yet see more windmills put back into service. There are said to be 10,000 of them, but even allowing for some exaggeration, you cannot count on seeing thousands of windmills with sails unfurled and spinning at any and all times. Much depends on the time of year you come and the time of day. If you would like the best chance, inquire at the National Tourist office in Iraklion and see what their best information is.

Even if the windmills are not in motion, it is an impressive sight. And by following the road all around the edge of the plain-through **Tzermiadhes**

and **Ayios Constantinos-**you come to the village of **Psykhro,** which is the base for visiting the **Dhiktaion Cave.** You can drive up to a parking area that is a short walking distance to the cave, and probably most people will want to hire one of the local guides who are available. They offer support for the descent down a rather tricky and slippery approach and also provide light and basic identifications of the parts of the cave. (The whole visit from **Psykhro** requires at least an hour, much depending on the numbers of people ahead of you.)

The myth, as set down by the ancient poet **Hesiod,** was that **Cronus,** the early master-god of the earth, feared that one of his children would overthrow him, so he ate all those borne by his wife **Rhea.** When **Zeus** was born, however, she knew better-and so she gave **Cronus** a stone to eat and spirited the baby Zeus

Plains of Lasithoi with their famous windmills

away to be reared in still another Cretan Cave, on Idha (p. 54). Obviously it is hard to prove just which cave Zeus was born in, but this one was definitely used as a cult shrine from Minoan times on. Eventually it got covered over, but by the 1880s it was rediscovered by local men who called it to the attention of archaeologists.

It is not that big as caves go, but the mythological and historical associations lend it resonance. You will be shown one large stalactite that is called "the mantle of Zeus" (that is, his swaddling cloth) and one small side chamber that is claimed as the actual birthing room because so many ancient votive offerings were found there. Zeus's birthplace or not, it can be a moving experience to pay homage to such an age-old shrine.

ARKHANES

This is a town in the mountains south of Iraklion that until recent years was known primarily as the center of a productive and progressive agricultural region. But since the 1960s, a series of quite dramatic archaeological finds have made international headlines for **Arkhanes** and marked it as one of the critical sites of Minoan culture.

You drive to Arkhanes by the Knossos road-some 2 km. past the palace, on the right, noting the remains of an aqueduct that arches a ravine; it is said to date only from the early 19th century. At about 9 km. from Iraklion center, where you must take the signposted turn to the right, is where the British and Cretan partisans flagged down and kidnapped the German commandant of Crete in World War II (p. 28). At 13 km., you have arrived at Arkhanes, and at the very edge of town, by a large school, you should see a sign pointing to the right for **Phourni**. You can drive several

Panayia Kera: A 16th Century church near Kritsa, St. Nicholas

Archanes: Necropolis at Anemospilia

hundred meters down and then up and around a very rough trail, but then you must leave the car and climb up a stony gully along the ridge that ascends the slope. At the top sits the great necropolis, or cemetery, of **Minoan Arkhanes.** It is now fenced in and you must ask at the National Tourist office in Iraklion as to who has the key and when you can visit it (and the temple at **Anemospilia,** below).

The tombs that have been excavated since the 1960s are fairly impressive as remains and have yielded some quite extraordinary objects -which you will see in Iraklion's museum: the skull of a bull and a horse's skeleton-sacrificed in honor of the notable Minoan woman buried in one of the tombs, considerable gold jewelry, ivory pieces, bronze vessels, and two iron beads (even rarer than gold in Minoan times). The tombs themselves constitute a museum of tomb types from about 2500 to 1300 B.C., and you can see the elaborate structures including domed tombs that this community was able to construct.

Indeed, the question raised by this cemetery has been: where did this community-especially its elite-live. Well, in the town of Arkhanes, just off to the left as you come to the divided one-way fork, is the beginning of what is presumed to be the "palace" of Minoan Arkhanes. Evans was the first to suggest that this site might yield an impressive structure, but it has remained to recent years for the major excavating to proceed (partly hampered by the presence of inhabited homes over the site).

But it was in 1979 that Arkhanes "exploded" on the horizon of Minoan archaeology. A husband and wife team of archaeologists had been excavating the Arkhanes sites, and a field survey by **Mrs. Sakellarakis** revealed some finds that led them to dig on a remote promontory, to the west of the town, a place known as **Anemospilia**-"the wind caves". What was found was a relatively small Minoan structure, but unusual because it was a temple (as indicated by finds of a cult statue, ritual vases, and such). But what was most amazing was the presence of four skeletons in the temple-obviously caught there when 53 the temple collapsed on them, presumably during some strong earthquake. Three of the skeletons were in one small chamber, and from various finds and careful deduction, Sakellarakis was forced to conclude that a young man was being sacrificed by a priest at the very moment they all were trapped. (The third person in the chamber seems to have been at attendant woman, while the fourth person was caught while in an adjacent corridor — evidently bearing a ritual vase associated with sacrifices.) It seemed to make sense: realizing that a great earthquake was imminent, they had chosen to sacrifice this youth — but they were too late to appease the gods.

Many scholars, especially Greek's, strongly resisted this interpretation of the finds. But in fact there has long been engaged in some sacrifice of humans. You need not get involved in the scholars' controversies, but if you have a taste for seeking out such sites, you can drive up to the temple. The view alone will reward you-and help to confirm that this temple was placed here for a very special reason: you feel as though you could mediate between earth and heaven. The temple is now fenced in, so you would have to see about the key (as indicated above, for the **Phourni** cemetery). The ride takes you out of the side of the town of Arkhanes and up the asphalt road to the town dump (marked with small blue & white signs); another km. or so beyond the dump (and the road is now dirt), you come to a bend-and there on your left is the temple.

54   If you enjoy tracking down

such sites, you might also like to visit a Minoan "manor-house" at **Vathypetro**, about 7 km. beyond Arkhanes on the road leading south; again, the interesting utensils-an oil press and wine press-are kept in a locked shelter so you would have to inquire about the key. Yet another possibility if you have come this far is to drive up to the top of **Mt. Iouktas**, the peak that resembles a recumbent head and is said to be that of the buried Zeus. The road is a turn off to the right (signposted) at about 3 km. south of Arkhanes; and it is another 3 km. up a solid dirt road. There is not that much to see up there-an **Orthodox chapel**, a radio transmitter-but the view over the countryside to Iraklion is quite dramatic.

FODHELE: EL GRECO'S BIRTHPLACE

A change from archaeological sites is offered by an excursion to **Fodhele**, the village that has been generally conceded to have the best claim to be the birhtplace of **Domenico Theotokopoulos**. (This claim is based largely on references to this family name in documents contemporary with the artist.) The village itself is not especially attractive as Cretan villages go, but many people enjoy paying homage to this distinctive son of Crete-El Greco.

You have a choice of several ways to go there. One is by the old road that turns off at 7 km. west of Iraklion and goes up over **Rogdhia** and **Akhlada** and then descends to **Fodhele**. Another possibility is to remain on the old road that goes west from Iraklion, and after climbing into the hills, turn

right at the 20 km. point and descend to Fodhele. Yet another possibility is to get onto the new national highway at Iraklion and head west and at 22 km, take the signposted turnoff to Fodhele.

Fodhele today is best known for its oranges. But the village takes some pride in showing visitors the remains of an old house off in a field that they claim was **El Greco's** birth home in 1541. The priest at the chapel in the village also keeps some reproductions of El Greco's works. And there is a small monument to El Greco placed in the village center by the **University of Valladolid of Spain,** El Greco's adopted land. There are other places around Iraklion that make claims to being associated with El Creco-such as the **School of the Mt. Sinai** monks at what is now **Ayia Katerina** in Iraklion (p. 32). But Fodhele should do for those who want to make a pilgrimage to this artist's home.

IDHA CAVE
VIA TYLISSOS
& ANOYIA

This is a day's excursion that offers something for everyone-a bit of archaeology, some contemporary village life, and a cave with strong mythological and historical associations. The archaeology is to be seen at **Tylissos**, where three Minoan villas have been excavated. The village is **Ano-yia**, which has turned itself into a "typical" Cretan village for tourists but has at least kept up some of the old handicrafts. And the cave is **Idha,** said to be where Zeus was raised to hide him from the furious Cronus (p. 51) and which became a major cult center.

You leave Iraklion by the old road to the west, and start the climb up into the foothills, but at 11 km. you take the (signposted) turn to the left for **Tylissos.** In the village of Tylissos, you follow the signs to the Minoan villas (which keeps regular visiting hours). The three houses are hardly dramatic, but they serve to remind us that not all Minoans even the privileged elite, lived in palaces. Strolling through these villas-noting the stairs and rooms and columns and painted plaster-you can feel the more modest dimensions of Minoan life. (The three large cauldrons in **Iraklion's museum-Room VII**-came from **Tylissos.** Made of bronze, the largest weighs 49 kilos). The round structure with the stairway at its side, by the way, is from the post-destruction or **Late Minoan period;** it is a cistern, and its feeder pipes connected to a spring that still supplies water to Tylissos.

Leaving Tylissos, you drive on the road out of the village (not back in the direction you came from) until after some 22 km. you have climbed up to 55

Anoyia, on the slopes of the **Idha Mountains.** During **World War II, Anoyia** was one of several Cretan villages singled out by the German occupation forces for retaliation after the German commandant was kidnapped (p. 25): all the males who could be caught were killed and most of the buildings (except the church) were razed. Perhaps to express their determination not to be obliterated, the people of Anoyia not only rebuilt their village but worked to revive some of the traditional crafts- particularly weaving woolens. Then, when tourists began to seek out Anoyia to purchase woolen rugs and bags, the village also began to provide more elaborate services. Now it is one of several Cretan villages that provides a "Crete by Night" excursion: food and drink, with some local people performing traditional music and dances.

But if you have come for the day, you now turn south out of Anoyia and climb some 18 km. up a winding mountain road until you come up onto the **Nidha Plain,** another of Crete's large upland plains. You can drive up to a restaurant and then there is a 20 minute walk up to the **Idha Cave.** (The summit of the **Idha Mountains, Timios Stavros,** involves a long hike and should not be attempted without a guide). The cave itself is not all that spectacular, but once again it is its associations that make it impressive. The finds- including superb bronze shields now in **Iraklion's Museum (Room XII)** - indicate that this cave was the center of a cult for the **Dorian Greeks,** a cult that seems to have honored the **Curetes,** the warriors who danced round the cave when the infant Zeus was being raised here and by their clashing schields drowned out the god's cries from the jealous Cronus.

Aghia Paraskevi village. Psyloritis Mt. in the background.

Typical Cretan Wearing

MALLIA

Mallia was long identified with one landmark, the third of the great Minoan palaces. But in recent years it has become one of the more popular and developed beach resorts. A day's excursion from Iraklion would allow you time to enjoy both Mallias as well as several other points of interest enroute to or from.

You take the new road east out of Iraklion, and those who are not that interested in archaeology may want to drive the straight 35 km to Mallia. But a detour just on the edge of Iraklion would allow a visit to three interesting places with Minoan associations. (Two of them-**the Cave of Eileithyia** and **Nirou Khani** are kept locked; the caretaker for both has been in **Nirou Khani,** but inquire at the National Tourist office in Iraklion to see what the present arrangements are.) What you must do is leave the new highway right after the airport and turn left down onto the old coast road. Depending where you come out, you may have to turn left and head back a short distance toward Iraklion-in any case, follow the signs to **Amnissos** and **Episkopi. Amnissos** is down on the beach, and is believed to have been the port of **Knossos;** the remains of the buildings there are thus considered the port authority's headquarters. (**Idomeneus,** the leader of the Cretan contingent to the **Trojan war,** set sail from here.) **Amnissos** has become well known in Minoan archaeology for being the place where **Spyridon Marinatos,** excavating in the 1930s, found the pumice from the **Santorini** volcanic explosion and thus was led to propose that it was this cataclysm that had brought a dramatic end to Minoan civilization.

But a far more interesting locale to visit is the **Cave of Eileithyia,** just about 2 km up 57 the climbing road toward **Episkopi;** a small sign on the left indicates the location, and a fig tree marks the cave's entrance. As a symbol of fertility, the fig tree is appropriate here because Eileithyia was a goddess of "freedom"-in this usage, freedom from pain in childbirth. From well before 3000 B.C. and even to this day, the cave has been frequented by local people who left their offerings and said their prayers in hopes of Eileithyia's aid. You can only walk back, about 50 meters into the cave-although you will still want some illumination-but it can be one of the most suggestive experiences if you are sensitive to such places. Perhaps it will add to your appreciation to know that this very cave is referred to in the **Odyssey** (Book XIX).

Now, if you have detoured to visit Amnissos or the cave, you stay on the old coast road and head east. (Offshore is **Dia Islet,** the major preserve of the Cretan wild goat: see p. 15). At about 13 km. you come to the edge of a settlement with the remains of the Minoan megaron of **Nirou Khani** at the very right of the road. The remains themselves are not that impressive, but there were important finds here-including the great bronze double axes (in **Room VII** of **Iraklion's museum**) - suggesting that this building served as the distribution center for religious and ritual objects.

Now continue east-passing at about 16 km. the **American Air Force Station**-and about 17 km, this old road merges with the new road. You continue on until about 27 km. you reach

Limin Khersonisou, often known as **Khersonnisos.** This village has now been overwhelmed by touristic facilities-hotels, rooms to rent, restaurants, and gift shops-and you need not stop if you don't care for such a developed beach resort. (Down on the waterfront, however, there is one curious remain: a pyramidal fountain from the Roman period. There are also some ancient remains to be seen underwater off the promontory at the west side of the modern settlement).

This whole road has been fairly well built up with touristic accommodations of one kind or another, and Mallia, at about 33 km., is simply the climax of this development, with its several large hotels and many smaller ones. But the beaches are good here, so you might like to leave time for a swim and a meal. The palace itself is at a turnoff some 4 km. east of the village. (It is fenced and observes regular visiting hours but at least until the present has not charged admission.) Although originally excavated by a Cretan, this site was assigned to the French who have continued to dig here over the decades and are still revealing the extend of this site. The palace itself is neither as big as **Knossos** nor as dramatically situated as **Phaestos,** but it rewards at least a stroll through its rooms and around the central court. It also offers several unique remains: in the middle of the court is a sacrificial pit (now covered over); beside the staircase at the far southwest corner of the center court is a round offering table, with 34 small recesses around its edge and a larger

depression in the center: although offering stones are familiar from Minoan sites, this is the only one with this patterns of hollows. And off to the southwest corner of the palace are eight large stone-walled pits-several with the bases of the roof-supporting pillars in the center: it is believed that these were storage silos. And no one leaves **Mallia** without posing for a picture beside one of the giant **pithoi!**

OTHER EXCURSIONS FROM IRAKLION

The main excursions described in no way exhaust the possibilities of the countryside around Iraklion, let alone the center of Crete conveniently reached from Iraklion. There are countless small villages, many with some distinctive structures or atmosphere. There are many more archaeological and historical landmarks. There are the numerous churches and chapels and monasteries. There are remote mountain slopes-and beaches

both secluded and developed. Always, too, there are the pleasures of the journeys themselves-the natural landscape, the unexpected encounters. There is something for every taste and every ambition.

PHAESTOS WITH GORTYNA AND MATALA

A visit to the second-most impressive of the Minoan palaces, **Phaestos,** has traditionally been the second-most popular excursion for visitors to Crete. It can be done in a day's roundtrip from Iraklion-in fact, many people from cruise ships fit it into the same day with **Knossos** and the museum! But if you visit only the Minoan palace, you miss a whole range of interesting sights along the route and around **Phaestos.** There is now a decent selection of overnight accommodation on the southern coast, too, so that you could stay there and then head either east (to **Ierapetra, Ayios**

A tourist shop in Mallia .

A Pithos in Mallia

Nikolaos, Sitia, and **Zakros**) or west to **Rethymnon** and **Khania**.

Whatever your eventual destination, you leave Iraklion by the **Khania Gate** and follow the road south (away from the coast and not the east-west new higway) through the fertile vineyards and then slowly begin the ascent along the edge of the **Idha Mountains.** At 28 km. you arrive at the village of **Ayia Varvara**: the large rock balanced near the beginning of the village is called the **omphalos,** or "navel" of Crete, as it is said to be the exact midpoint of the island. At the other end of the village, a turn to the left (signposted) would lead to a worthwhile detour for those with a bit of time. At about 20 km from this turn, a right turn leads up a steep hill to the **Monastery of Vrondisi**; it boasts an unexpectedly **Italianate fountain,** fine frescoes in its **Church of Ayios Antonios,** and some valuable old ikons formerly in the **Church of Ayios Fanourios,** just a few kilometers further on. This church should be visited by all interes-ted in **Byzantine art,** for it has some interesting architectural elements, as well as some of the finest frescoes (dating from the 14th and 15th centuries). And still another couple kilometers on would bring you to the village of **Kamares,** the starting point for a climb to the cave of that name, now memorialized as a style of thin, polychrome Minoan pottery that was first discovered in the cave.

Proceeding south out of **Ayia Varvara,** you are soon driving along the pass that brings you through to the edge of the **Messara,** Crete's largest plain. It extends about 25 km. on its east-west axis, and is about 5 km. wide. Obviously, it has long been the island's major agricultural area, but because it has been so divided up among families, and because it has had something of a water shortage, it was never as productive as it might have been. Now it is better irrigated, and there is some cooperation with sharing fields and farm machinery. The Minoans found it first, and the Romans

A new of the remains of the Palace in Mallia

intended it to be one of their granaries; modern Cretans will certainly make something more from this natural resource.

At 44 km. you have descended to the village of **Ayii Dheka** - "the holy ten," in reference to ten inhabitans of this area who refused to abandon their Christian faith for the Roman gods and so were beheaded. The local chapel contains what is said to be the graves of the martyrs. You continue on the main road for a couple of kilometers until you pull off to the right at the great **Basilica of Ayios Titos** at **Gortyna,** a site that figures prominently in three phases of Crete's history. Going backwards in time, it was here that one **Titus** seems to have served as the leader of Crete's first Christians; whether **Paul** actually came to **Gortyna** or sent Titus here, he certainly wrote an epistle to Titus. It was fitting, then, that this first great **Christian basilica** on Crete was dedicated to **Titus** (to this day, the patron saint of the island): the remains you visit date from the 6th to 10th centuries.

But the reason this was such

The remains of the Theatre in Gortyn

an active Christian community is that it had earlier been selected by the Romans to serve as their capital of the province that included Crete and **Cyrene** (in North Africa, across from Crete). The **Romans** made **Gortyna** into a quite ambitious provincial city, and its remains are now scattered around the fields and olive groves opposite the basilica. There is a stadium, a theater, several temples and sanctuaries, and a great many statues-nothing very aesthetically pleasing but the type of site that inevitably prompts visitors to speculate on the transience of human endeavours: to find a Roman imperial capital in a remote field on Crete...

The Romans' choice of this site as their capital was not a random one. And this introduces the first phase of Gortyna's role in history. The Dorian Greeks who moved into Crete sometimes after 1100 B.C. made Gortyna into their most dynamic city-state, so that from about 800 B.C. on it was developing a society much like that of the better known **Dorians of Sparta.** What Gor-

Law Code of Gortyn inscribed in 500 B.C. in the Dorian dialect

The Church of St. Titus in Gortyn

tyna did that was unique, however, was to record its laws on a monumental inscribed wall. This is the famous **Law Code of Gortyna,** now to be seen in an enclosed area behind the **Roman Odeon.** Dating from about 500 BC, the inscription has over 17,000 characters recording an archaic Doric Greek; they are written in the so-called ox-plow manner-running from right to left, then left to right, in alternating lines. Most of the text deals with civil law-marriage, property rights, adoption, and such. This code (found scattered in a stream in the late 19th century) has proven of inestimable value to students of this era of Greek history.

Proceeding on along the road (now heading west) you pass through the market town of **Mires** and come at 60 km. to the turn left (signposted) to **Phaestos,** crowning the hill. In fact, it is hard to believe that such a site could ever have been buried, but most of it was until Italian archaeologists began to excavate it at the same time Evans was digging at Knossos. The Italians have also continued their excavations to this day, but unlike Evans, they chose to do very little reconstruction. Still, there is enough standing to give a fine impression of this magnificent palace-and above all, there is its location, riding the crest like the prow of a ship, with the **Messara** spread out below and the **Idha Mountains** off to the north.

The palace can be visited during regular hours-it can be withering hot in the midday sun! Most of what you see belongs to the second of the palaces (as is true at Knossos), but remains of not only the first palace but many other eras are around. Phaestos has many of the familiar architectural elements of the Minoan palaces, but it also has several distinctive features. Its west court, or theatral area, which 63 you come down onto by a narrow flight of stairs, was probably used for ceremonial processions, while the eight broad stairs along one side were used as seats. The **Grand Staircase** is just that-a truly monumental flight of stairs. The **Central Court** is smaller than that at Knossos, but its setting makes it at least as impressive. All around it are the various administrative, ritual, and residential quarters. You will want to investigate the storerooms on the block extending off the northwest corner. And you will certainly want to explore the whole north wing, with its quite elaborate rooms assumed to have been used by the royal family. One unusual element is a furnace used for pottery or metal working on the raised area just above the northeast corner.

Those with more time must now decide which of the several nearby attractions they want to visit.

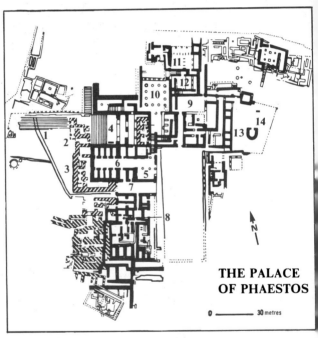

**THE PALACE
OF PHAESTOS**

0 ——————— 30 metres

1 West Court
2 First Palace
3 West Façade
4 Propylaion
5 A square Pillard Hall
6 Magazines
7 A Corridor

8 A lustral Basin
9 Internal Court
10 Peristyle Hall
11 King's Room
12 Queen's Room
13 Workshops
14 A Large Furnace

The remains of the Central Court in Phaestos

SIDE EXCURSIONS FROM PHAESTOS

After you have visited Phaestos - and possibly enjoyed a meal at the **Tourist Pavilian** overlooking the palace - you have numerous possibilities depending on your time and interests. Assuming that you do have more time, you might like to visit the satellite villa of

The Theatre and the Grand Staircase in the West Court area.

Phaestos known as **Ayia Triadha.** (It is famous among other reasons because the unique sarcophagus - in Room XIV in Iraklion's museum - was found in a nearby tomb.) You have three ways of getting there: one along the road on the ridge behind the Phaestos site, going essentially west until you come above Ayia Triadha; another way is to go down off the Phaestos hill as you came, turn left onto the main road, and drive about a km. until you see the posted turn to the left, that brings you in below Ayia Triadha; and it has even been possible to walk-about 45 minutes-along the north slope of the promontory between the two sites.

Not that Ayia Triadha is all that impressive-especially after Phaestos. But like many miniatures, it seems more accessible, more human-proportioned. Exactly what its relationship to Phaestos, so close, is still debated by the experts: a summer palace? occasional retreat? ritual center? a prince's little realm? By late Minoan times, at least, it had a regular settlement right alongside (to the north), with a whole line of storage bays or shops. The Mycenaeans seem to have built one of their megarons right smack over the middle of the earlier Minoan structure. Perhaps most enjoyable are the rooms that sit at the west end-a terrace, a colonnaded men's hall, and the queen's hall with its gypsum benches and walls lined with alabaster. Since these rooms have a view out over the sea, and it is believed that the coast was much closer to the villa in Minoan times, it has been suggested that this was a sort of seaside villa (which any Greek who can afford it still likes to maintain).

After Ayia Triadha, you deserve a break from archaeology, so it is time to go down to **Matala,** the legendary "cove of the caves". From Ayia Triadha you must go back to the Phaestos and down the other (south) side. At about the 2 km. point from Phaestos, you pass on your left the fascinating 14th - century **Chapel of Ayios Pavlos,** seemingly rooted in the soil. Continuing on and skirting the village of **Pitsidia,** you pass at about the 7,5 km. point a dirt trail to the right that leads down to **Kommo:** this site has long been known to have something there, and it has been claimed as the port of Minoan Phaestos, but only starting in the late 1970s have excavations confirmed that this is indeed an ambitious site. But you want to keep on the road and wind down to arrive at 12 km. at Matala. If you can see beyond the

tavernas and beach crowds, you will see what has made this place: two arms that enfold a cove, the arms made of a semi-hard sandstone that Cretans have been able to dig rooms into over the centuries. They really are more like rooms, too, than caves: some are practically suites, with "built-in" bunks. Exactly when Cretans began to do this is not known; perhaps since Roman times at the earliest. But from the mid-1960s to the early 70s, Matala was adopted by the international Hippy movement, and they used it as one of their main stops on their migrations. But the whole place got so dirty and crowded (there were no real toilet facilities) that the authorities forbade anyone to live or sleep in the rooms. They can be inspected, though, and the beach is decent, and there are some tavernas and basic overnight accommodations, so it might be worth a day's visit.

After Matala, there are still more choices. Just over the cape to the east-but accessible only by a long drive from the Messara-is **Kaloi Limenes,** the "fair havens", according to some, mentioned in the **Bible** (Acts XXVII:8) as the port where **Paul** put in. Then, still farther east along that coast-but also accessible by another road-is the site of Leben, known throughout the ancient Greek world (6th-3rd centuries BC at least) for its curative waters. Its temple was thus dedicated to **Asclepius,** god of medicine, and remains-including a sea-horse mosaic-are to be seen. And the whole of the Messara is dotted with remains

Ancient rock cut tombs in the clifts at Matala harbor of Gortyn.

of early Minoan tombs.

For many people, though, the goal will be **Ayia Galini,** on the coast to the northwest of Matala. You go back to the main road below Phaestos or **Ayia Triadha** and continue west, passing through **Timbaki,** which has an unpretentious beach on the edge of town. You continue on, climb a bit, then bear left and descend to the coast and come (in 19 km from Phaestos) to Ayia Galini. Up until about 1970 it was a rather secluded and undistinguished little port that rose up the steep slopes from the sea. Young people, however, found it and soon the word spread-

and now all of Europe seems to want a room in Ayia Galini. It still has no particular attractions-not even the charm of **Cycladic** ports-and it can get overcrowded. But many people claim to like Ayia Galini for at least a short stay. Look it over, and if you don't like it go back to Timbaki or on to Rethymnon (on the north coast-a relatively short drive over the mountains).

EASTERN CRETE

The eastern end of the island has long drawn visitors with its mixture of distinctive attractions-a great international chic

Fishing boats

esort, the one complete Minoan town, a palace excavated as in some modern fairytale, and a tropical palm beach. All these could be passed through in one long day from Iraklion, but to really see them, and other points of interest, most people will want to base themselves in eastern Crete. **Ayios Nikolaos, Sitia,** or **Ierapetra** would be the more obvious bases. Perhaps arrive during the late afternoon and be in position to get an early start in the morning; alternatively, set out early from Iraklion and end up in one of these towns early in the evening. Also, **Sitia and Ayios Nikolaos** are ports of entry or exit from or to **Rhodes** and **Santorini,** so eastern Crete might be combined with plans for one or other of those islands. However you arrive, you should allow at least two days for eastern Crete.

Most people probably still head east from Iraklion. You have the choice of turning down onto the old coast road (with possible visits to **Amnisso, the Cave of Eileithyia,** and **Nirou Khania:** described on pp. 57), or you can stay on the new highway$_6$ until it merges with the old (as indicated on p. 57). You then pass through **Khersonnisos** and **Mallia** (as described on pp. 58 60) after which you continue east. At some 5 km. after the Mallia turnoff you pass, on your right, the **Monastery of Selinaris,** up on the rocky slope: it has long been traditional to travelers to stop and get the protection of **St. George.** You proceed on, and most people will probably stay on the new highway, for the mountain road has no special landmarks. The new highway, furthermo-

Mallia beach

re, has its own appeal, what with miles of flowering bushes lining the road. In another 10 km. you are passing the edge of **Neapolis,** a provincial town that claims the courts for eastern Crete, its almond-drink, **soumadha** (p. 102), and the birthplace of **Peter Philargos** who became **Pope Alexander V** in 1409.

Most people will not detour, probably, but will drive the next 15 km. on the highway straight to **Ayios Nikolaos.**

AYIOS NIKOLAOS

A quiet, picturesque harbor-town until the mid-1960s, **Ayios Nikolaos** was selected to be the center for some of the most ambitious resorts and hotels on Crete. In their wake, inevitably, came the chic shops, restaurants, and cafes, along with everything else required by modern tourism. As such places go, Ayios Nikolaos has developed with some style and restraint, and although you will now find yourself sitting next to foreigners, you can still sit around the harbor and watch the world go by. There are some good beaches around the bay, and for those who can afford them the resorts at Ayios Nikolaos and **Elounda** are superb for their class.

Ayios Nikolaos is a somewhat artificial town in the first place, as it has largely been built up by "emigrants" from elsewhere on Crete and the harbor was formed by isolating the so-called bottomless pool behind the port. Otherwise known as **Lake Voulismeni**, it seems to be fed by some underground spring or stream so that it is a freshwater that gets diluted by the sea when the currents change. It has been measured to the depth of 64 meters. At the far side the town maintains a small collection of animals. The only place that you might feel obligated to visit is the **Archaeological Museum,** which has been growing in recent years because of the various excavations in eastern Crete. Perhaps its most intriguing display is the "**goddess of Myrtos,**" a ceramic figure of a woman with a water jug that somehow seems more modern than anything sold by the contemporary potters in town. It is Minoan and dates from perhaps 1500 BC.

Ayios Nikolaos

EXCURSIONS FROM AYIOS NIKOLAOS

The one sidetrip that almost everyone will want to take is up to **Kritsa,** with its impressive Byzantine - frescoed Church of **Panayia Kera**. It is an easy 10 km drive almost due south from **Ayios Nikolaos,** up in an olive grove on the right of the road, just before the village of **Kritsa** itself. In fact, it will be hard to miss it, there are usually so many buses and tourists there, but with a little patience you can find a time when the church is not quite so crowded. The church itself presents a striking exterior. Inside its three naves are all more or less covered with frescoes dating from the 15th and 16th centuries; with close inspection you should be able to make out many familiar episodes from the Biblical accounts of the life of the Virgin Mary and of Christ. The frescoes have been considerably restored, but they are still regarded as a strong example of Byzantine art. Two other churches in the neighborhood of **Kritsa - Ayios Ioannis** and **Ayios Georgios** - also have fine frescoes.

If you have come this far you might at least go up to the village of Kritsa, a pleasant mountain village that has kept up its work in textiles. Kritsa also happens to be the village used as the locale for the film version of **Kazantzakis' Greek Passion** - the French film (with local actors), **He Who Must Die.**

Also up in this area is the site of **Lato**, with its quite impressive Hellenistic remains spread around the slopes and enjoying a magnificent view out over the **Gulf of Merebello.** The road to Lato is off to the right, just before entering the

Elounda beach

Gournia

village and past the cemetery.

A more popular excursion from Ayios Nikolaos is by small boat to **Spinalonga Island,** in the gulf to the north. The Venetians had constructed one of their major forts on this islet by 1579, but eventually it fell to the Turks. After they gave it over early in this century, it was turned into a leper colony. That was long ago dispersed, and now tourists wander about its derelict and atmospheric remains.

Across from Spinalonga Islet is the village of **Elounda** and connected to that by an isthmus is the peninsula of Spinalonga with some remains from the **Doric Greek** and Hellenistic periods, including a mosaic with dolphins. Elounda and these remains, known as ancient **Olous,** are reached by road from Ayios Nikolaos; the salt flats you pass going out to the peninsula are attributed to some French engineers in the late 19th century.

GOURNIA

This site involves a drive of about 20 km from **Ayios Nikolaos,** but whether you are going on to see other points in the east or not, this is worth a special trip. For on an island where Minoan "palaces" are becoming commonplace, this is the exception that ends up surprising many visitors: a well-preserved, if small, Minoan town. It sits on a low rise at about the narrowest point on Crete, which may account for its presence: ships may have been off-loaded here and the goods carried overland to avoid the long voyage around the eastern end of the island. In any case, **Gournia** seems to have been a functioning town, and you can walk up and down its streets and peer into house after house. All that survives are the ground floors; it is believed that people climbed up to second stories by outside steps. At the high point is the "palace" of the local ruler, but this gives the wrong impression, for it is little more than a large house. What strikes most visitors, in fact, is how small the houses are-but many people around the world to this day live in very small rooms. The finds from **Gournia** (now on display in **Iraklion's Museum**) further confirm that this was a working community. One final claim to distinction: Gournia was the first major archaeological excavation supervised by a woman: between 1901-4, **Harriet Boyd** from the **United States.**

If you have the time and are heading east, you continue on from Gournia (not failing to look back from the opposite hill to get a fine view over the site) and come down to the next village, **Pakhia Ammos**. Just outside of this is a turn to the right that leads to **Ierapetra** and the south coast. Save that diversion for later (p. 78) and proceed east along the winding and often spectacular coast road (all new) that has earned this stretch the name of "**the Riviera of Crete**". (Don't plan to eat on this stretch, because there is next to nothing to be had.) It is some 3 km. from Gournia before you have dscended down to itia on the coast.

Mosque in Ierapetra

SITIA AND EXCURSIONS

Sitia is a relatively quiet port town that is only beginning to expand its hotel and restaurant capacity to accommodate the growing numbers who keep seeking out such undiscovered places. The town itself provides almost no distractions other than some fine swimming and the pleasures of sitting along the waterfront and eating. The remains of the Venetian fort are disappointing and the churches are undistinguished. Perhaps **Sitia** will remain just what it is, a place to eat and sleep in while enroute to other places.

One of those places has been the **Monastery** of **Toplou,** about 20 km. east of Sitia (with the turn off to the left at the 15 km point). The present structure dates from the 17th century (and has recently undergone a major restoration). It appears almost like a fort and its name is from a Turkish word, **top,** for cannon, for it was reputed to be armed with one. It is a prosperous monastery, owning much land in the area. On the facade of its chapel, in the cramped inner court, is a plaque from the second century BC that records a treaty between two Cretan city-states, **Itanos** and **Ierapetra.** Within the chapel is one of the most celebrated ikons on Crete: the work of the 18th-century painter, **Ioannis Kornaros,** it is known as **"Great is the Lord"** for its depiction of the diversity and plenitude of the world.

If you were to visit Toplou, it is possible to take a road

Vaï

from there and cut off to the north and the outermost cape with the beach at **Vai**. But the road is not that good, and most people will probably prefer to rejoin the main road and proceed east to **Palaikastro,** there turning up to **Vai.** (Palaikastro itself has some Minoan remains down on the east coast, but they are of little interest except to specialists.) You will know when you are approaching **Vai** - from the stands of palm trees. These trees seem to have been here from time immemorial-whether planted by some early individuals or they took root after some seeds or root stock washed ashore. **Vai** can be lovely, but it has been overwhelmed by the sheer numbers who come to enjoy that loveliness. Go off season and you'll have a better chance of finding it more like a tropical paradise.

Monastery of Toplou

KATO ZAKROS

The destination for anyone at all interested in the Minoans and archaeology will be **Kato Zakros,** the seasonal settlement down on the southeast coast that has given its name to the fourth of the great Minoan palaces. It is a 46 km. drive from **Sitia**-and unfortunately there has been no bus service for the last 7 km.-east to **Palaikastro** and then south to **Ano Zakros** and down to the coast at **Kato Zakros**

The palace sits back from its small bay and in this respect it already differs from the other palaces, which do not seem to have been situated at working seaports. But **Zakros** was, as the more recent excavations are revealing: a whole port city is gradually emerging from the environs of the palace proper, and it is believed that more would be revealed had this part of the coast not subsided considerably. As it is, the road from the palace down to the harbor is clearly there.

The palace itself shares many of the same archaeological, historical, and architectural elements with the other three. It has its great center court, its administrative area, its residential area, its ritual sections, and its workshops and service rooms. It has some distinctive features, however such as the fountain-well and cistern in two adjacent rooms on the east side, off the midsection: spring water seems to have been brought up right here and then distributed throughout the palace. Another distinctive aspect is that it appears that the residents had enough advance warning of some impending disaster - presumably an earthquake - to

Vaï Beach on the North Easternmost part of Crete

grab their personal belongings and flee; the palace was then destroyed quite thoroughly, burying a great many artifacts so completely that the remote site was never plundered. The rich finds are to be seen primarily in **Room VIII** in **Iraklion's Museum.**

But the whole site takes on a special dimension when you know the story of its discovery. A British archaeologist had actually revealed a few remains on the hill above the palace in 1901, but he abandoned the site. Apparently, though, a workman who assisted him found a gold necklace at that time, and hid it. Decades later he finally gave it to Dr. **Giamalakis** (p. 34), who in turn called it to the attention of **Prof. Nicholas Platon,** curator of **Iraklion's Museum** and head of excavations on Crete. He remained suspicious that a gold item like this might mean a palace, and meanwhile had written in the guide to the

museum that there were still important remains to be dug on Crete. Mr. and Mrs. **Leon Pomerance,** an American couple who had for many years been interested in art and archaeology, came across this claim while visiting the museum in 1960. They wrote and invited **Prof. Platon** to dig one of those sites and offered to support the work with a generous sum. **Platon** accepted and sunk his first trench in 1961-and thus launched an excavation that would go on until the present. The **Pomerances** continued their support for many years and out of this unique joint undertaking the impossible happened: a great **Minoan palace** and its contents were brought to light.

After you have visited Kato Zakros, you have several possibilities. You can go back to Sitia or Ayios Nikolaos (and even Ano, or Upper, Zakros has a small hotel), or you can go back to Pakhia 77

Ammos (50 km. from Sitia) and take the turn south to Ierapetra (another 16 km).

IERAPETRA AND EXCURSIONS

Like so many Cretan towns, **Ierapetra** underwent a transformation in the 1960s, from a sleepy backwater community to a bustling, expansive center. Ierapetra owes some of this change to having been adopted by young people as a pleasant (and cheap) retreat from 20-century pressures, but the people of Ierapetra were more interested in joining the 20th century. They began to plants tomatoes, cucumbers, and other vegetables under large plastic-covered greenhouses in order to provide produce for the tables of Western and Northern Europe throughout the winter months. This also required an ambitious collection and transportation system, so that the whole coast around Ierapetra is now organized to grow and harvest and truck out these vegetables. Ierapetra has prospered as a result, and meanwhile increasing numbers of tourists have sought it out.

The town of **Ierapetra** must be very old, possibly going back to Minoan times (when it was the southern link in the overland route between **Gournia:** see p. 72). But there are no remains from these early times, and only a few Roman pieces survive. There is a Venetian fort worth inspecting, and a Turkish minaret and fountain. There is also a house where it is claimed that **Napoleon** spent a night enroute to **Egypt.** The **Town Library** maintains a small collection of antiquities,

its prize being a superb **Minoan** sarcophagus. Mostly, though, people enjoy Ierapetra for its mild winter weather and its lazy waterfront.

If you were to base yourself here, you could drive west some 15 km. to **Myrtos,** itself a modest village that has been popular with young people looking for a cheap place to pass a warm winter. On peaks just east of **Myrtos** are two Minoan sites excavated since the late 1960s - **Pyrgos** and **Fournou Korifi** (or known locally as **Trouli**). Each has interesting remains considering their remote location.

From Myrtos it is possible to continue driving west up along the edge of the **Dhikti Mountains** via **Ano Viannos** (some 25 km. from Myrtos); all this is asphalt road, but soon after there is a bad stretch when you must turn off at **Martha** (10 km after Ano Viannos) and proceed down through **Skinias.** By this time, though, you are at the eastern end of the **Messara** (p. 61), and the road is in the process of being covered in asphalt, so you have a relatively easy drive west to join the road from **Iraklion** to **Phaestos** near **Ayii Dheka** (p. 62)-85 km. altogether from **Myrtos.**

Heading east from Ierapetra, there are some fine and relatively undiscovered beaches along the coast. At **Koutsouras** (some 24 km. east) there is a "touristic village" up on the slopes-an abandoned village whose houses have been converted into houses for rent. You could continue east and then north via **Lithines** and on up to **Sitia,** a total of 57 km. from Ierapetra.

Ierapetra harbour

WESTERN CRETE

The western half of the island has never attracted as many foreigners as the central and eastern parts - originally because it lacks the major archaeological sites, and more recently because it has not yet undergone the ambitious touristic developments. But all this makes the western half that much more appealing to many people. And there are some distinctive attractions-unexpected Venetian Renaissance and baroque buildings, unexpected Turkish - Islamic structures, many Byzantine churches and frescoes, a monastery that once became an international symbol of Cretans' dedication to freedom. And perhaps the most impressive natural attraction on the island-the **Gorge** of **Samaria.**

You could visit a fair amount of western Crete on a long day's excursion from **Iraklion–Khania** is only a two-hour drive on the new highway. But this would be hurried sightseeing. To visit and experience even a selection of places you should allow at least two days. And since Khania is a point of entry and exit for both ships (from Piraeus) and planes (from Athens), you could combine your visit to the west with your general itinerary in Greece. (There has also been a ship that connects **Kastelli,** west of **Khania,** with **Kythera** and the **Peloponnesos** enroute to and from Piraeus, yet another alternative).

Most people still approach the west from Iraklion, so this route is here described. If you join the new highway immedi-ately outside Iraklion, you can get to Rethymnon in about an hour; the scenery is quite spectacular, but you will not get a chance to see much else (except there is the turn-off to **Fodhele:** see p. 54). The old road goes up and along the **Idha Mountains**-about 80 km to **Rethymnon,** but requiring closer to two hours because of the curves and inclines and villages. If you were to take this route, you could make a detour to visit **Tylissos** (p. 55) and go on via **Anoyia** (p. 55), and then come down and rejoin the old road. At **Perama** (55 km) there is a turnoff to the right for **Melidhoni Cave** (about 6 km. toward the coast), one of several caves on Crete that have profound mythological and historical associations for all Cretans. Traditionally this is said to be the residence of **Talos,** the mythical bronze giant who protected the island by hurling boulders at undesirable approachers. (**Talos** shows up in the saga of the **Argonauts**-and also in **Dante's Inferno.**) Then in 1,24, after several hundred Cretans took refuge in the cave from marauding Turks, they were suffocated when the Turks set fire to the brushwood at the cave's mouth.

Just outside **Perama** is a turnoff to the left up to **Maragarites,** one of the villages that maintains the traditional pottery-making methods and styles (p. 99). But the most important detour on this road-and many people might prefer to get settled in Rethymnon and then drive back to it-is a turn-off at about 73 km (on this old road from Iraklion) at the village of **Platanies:** this leads in some 16 km. to the **Monastery of Arkadhi.**

The Front of the Church of the Arkadhi Monastery (1587)

MONASTERY OF ARKADHI

There are two surprises awaiting the foreigner who visits **Arkadhi.** One is the monastery church itself: with its elaborate facade (dated to 1587) it seems quite out of keeping with a Cretan monastery here in these remote hills; it is, in fact, a reminder of how the Venetians eventually came to influence much of Cretan architecture during their centuries here. But even before you enter the monastery courtyard you will have noted an impressive modern monument, with its busts and its ossuary: this is to honor those who died here in 1866, and

that episode's importance in history will be the other surprise.

Like so many of the monasteries throughout all of Greece, those of Crete had served as centers of both passive cultural maintenance and active resistance against the various foreign occupiers-particularly the Turks. In 1866, Cretans were once again trying to revolt against the Turks, and a large number of Cretans -women and children as well as fighters-had taken refuge in the monastery at Arkadhi. Surrounded by the Turks, they refused to surrender; instead, the story is, the abbot gave the command to blow up the powder magazine just as the

Turks stormed the walls-killing many hundreds (some versions say thousands) of Cretans and Turks. Word of this heroic and horrific episode soon reached the Western world and prompted many (including the French writer **Hugo**, the English poet **Swinburne**, the **Italian patriot Garibaldi**) to express their support for the Cretan cause (much as notables today support struggles for independence). The explosion occurred on November 9, and each year at this time there is a major celebration at Arkadhi and nearby Rethymnon to mark this great moment in Crete's long history.

Whether you have detoured to see Arkadhi or have come out from Rethymnon, you now proceed back down to the old east-west road and turn left toward Rethymnon, some 5 km. along the coast. (The new highway has not as of this writing bypassed Rethymnon, so it merges with the old road

Rethymnon

several kilometers east of here).

RETHYMNON

Third-largest city of Crete (yet only about 15,000 people), **Rethymnon** is yet another of the surprises and pleasures of the island. Because it never had the "pull" of **Khania** or **Iraklion,** it was by-passed by many historical developments, with the result that it retained more of its Venetian and Turkish pasts. It seems never to have been settled by the Minoans, and nothing much of its post-Minoan Greek phase survives. But the Venetians erected several structures, the most imposing being the great fort at the head of the promontory. Built over the site of earlier forts between 1573-80, this one is a superb example of the Italian fortifications of this era (and it has been fairly thoroughly restored in recent years); it also says something about such fortific-

ations that in the end the Turks merely came ashore down the coast and took over, rendering the fort irrelevant. The principal Venetian buildings within the fort fell into ruins; only a Turkish mosque now rewards those interested in architecture.

Elsewhere around town, however, are some interesting Venetian structures. The **Arimondi Fountain** is a curiosity, there are several churches, and many fine portals and architectural elements on various streets. The **Loggia**, dated to about 1600, is not much compared to Iraklion's, but it houses a small collection of antiquities from the region of **Rethymnon-Minoan, Hellenistic,** and **Roman.** The **Turks** generally took over **Venetian churches** and converted them into **mosques,** but they also built some mosques and erected minarets, and several of these are to be seen around town. Mostly, though, it is the narrow streets with their overhanging second-stories and carved woodwork that lend a Turkish flavor to the town. The last of **Rethymnon's Turks** were removed as part of the population exchange in the 1920s (see p. 22), and this episode features in a delightfull memoir of a Rethymnon boyhood by one of modern Greece's most distinguished writers, **Pandelis Prevelakis**-his **Tale of a Town.**

It is easy to lose yourself for a morning in strolling around Rethymnon and observing the contemporary as well as historical scene. There is then a fine public beach (with changing facilities and snacks) and a wide choice of eating places (including some around the small old harbor).

EXCURSIONS FROM RETHYMNON

Rethymnon certainly has enough fine hotels to allow you to use it as a base, but the

Arimondi Fountain in Rethymno

fact is that many of the attractions of its region are approached from **Iraklion**. A-yia Galini (p. 26) is actually in Rethymnon's nome, or district, as is **Anoyia** and the cave of **Idha** (p. 55). So, too, are **Melidhoni Cave** (p. 80) and the **Monastery of Arkadhi** (p. 24), described as detours en route from **Iraklion**. If you take the road up from Ayia Galini to Rethymnon, there are numerous chapels scattered throughout the hills with Byzantine frescoes. And the road passes through **Spili**, with its unusal Venetian fountain-17 lion-heads spouting water.

Some 9 km. north of Spili on this road is **Koxares**, where a turn to the west and drive south brings you down to the **Monastery of Preveli** (some 16 km. from Koxares). Ignore the old abandoned monastery and go on to the large 17th-century

10 C Venetian lion head fountains in Spili

Preveli overlooking the sea. It long served as a center of resistance against the **Turks**, and resumed that role in **World War II** when it helped to hide and then evacuate the many **British** and **Commonwealth** soldiers who got stranded on Crete after its fall to the **Germans** in 1941. There is a small museum and the monks are proud of a candelabra presented to them by grateful British troops after the war. West of **Preveli** is the pleasant beach at **Plakias** with adequate accommodations.

That will be about all most people would be able to see of Rethymnon and its district before heading farther west for **Khania**. Again, right outside Rethymnon you face the choice of the new or the old road. The new road goes right along the shore, with endless beaches, but there is not that much on the old road that will attract most people. However, at about 32 km. from Rethymnon on this old road there is a turn off to the left for **Lake Kournas**, the only freshwater lake on Crete. It is some 65 hectares in area and said to be quite deep, it has inspired many legends and it is certainly an unexpected and atmospheric phenomenon to encounter here. (Most unexpected is that no one has started a taverna on its shore.)

Still on the old road, you continue west and within a kilometer you are passing through **Georgioupolis** with its refreshing boulevard lined by eucalyptus trees. (These trees, which now seem so at home in Greece, were actually introduced here from **Australia** - as was the prickly pear cactus from **America**.) This village was named after the **Prince**

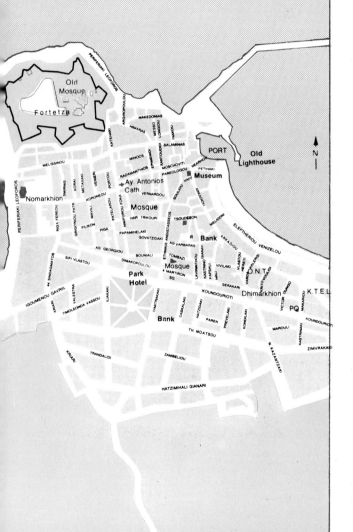

Rethimnon

0 ————————— 300 metres

Old Mosque

Fortetza

PERIFERIAKI LEOFOROS

ARGIROUPOLOU

KATEHAKI

MAKEDONIAS

HIMARAS

MESSO LONGIOU

EPIMENIDI

SALAMINAS

HANON

MOSCHOVITI

NEARHOU

PETIHAKI

PORT

Old Lighthouse

N

MELISSINOU

MINOOS

RADAMANTHOOS

KARITOUDIOU

SANTOUDIOU

MATSAKI

KRIARI / FEREOU

SMIRNIS

KORAI

VENIERI

PORTOU

METAXAKI

PIGA

NIKIFOROU FOKA

PAREOLOGOU

BOULIOU

VAFE

ARAMPATZOGLOU

Museum

Ay. Antonios Cath

VERNARDOU

Nomarkhion

PERIFERIAKI LEOFOROS

RIGS / FEREOU

GRIGORIOU PATH

MAVILI

PATELAROU

FILIKON

KORONEOU

Mosque

HAR TRIKOUPI

PAPAMIHELAKI

GOVATZIDAKI

TSOUDEBON

ETHNIKIS ANDISTASSEOS

AG VARBARAS

MELIDONI

ARKADIOU

ELEFTHERIOU VENIZELOU

Bank

AG. GEORGIOU

BOUNIALI

DIMAKOPOULOU

TOMBAZI

LAVIRINTHOU

DIMITRAKAKI

SIFI VLASTOU

44 SINDAGMATOS

VALESTRA

TIMOLEONDA VASSOU

ILIAMAKI

Park Hotel

MARTIRON SQ.

Mosque

KASTRINOU

GIANNI

ANTSAI

GERAKARI

VIVILAKI

VLASTOU

VARDA

MENETI

KOUNDOURIOTOU

VICTOR OUGNO

D.N.T.

Dhimarkhion

K.T.E.L.

IGOUMENOU GAVRIIL

KRIARI

DASKALAKI

HATZIDAKI

PAREN

KOUNDOURIOTI

KONOLAKI

PREVELAKI

MAKARDOU

PQ

KOUNDOURIOTI

Bank

TH. MOATSOU

MAROULI

N. KAZANTZAKI

KASTRINAKI

ZIMVRAKAKI

TRANDALIDI

ZAMBELIOU

HATZIMIHALI GIANARI

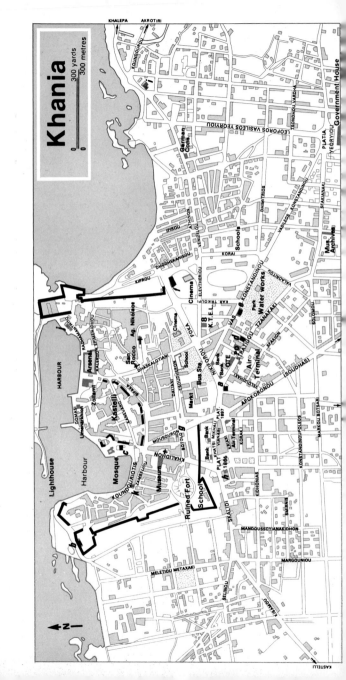

George played a role in Crete's independence struggles (p. 24). You could join the new highway here, or drive another 25 km. before doing so near **Kalives.** At that point, you are along the southeast shore of the great **Soudha Bay,** not only Crete's largest and most spectacular harbors but one of the largest in the Mediterranean. For that reason, it has been a major **NATO** naval base (which means that much of its shore is out of bounds for walking and photographing). Near the mouth of the bay is **Soudha Island,** with a **Venetian fort,** one of the last to surrender to the Turks (in 1715). Another 2 km. along the road and a turnoff to the left (to **Megala Khorafia/Aptera**) would bring you in about 3 km. to the remains of **Aptera.**

Aptera ("Featherless", from a mythical musical contest between the **Muses** and the **Sirens;** the Muses won so the Sirens removed their feathers and threw themselves into the bay) was quite an important city from the fifth century BC on through Roman times and into the early Christian era. The remains are scattered around the hilltop and have little interest, but the Turkish fort on the edge is fun to explore and offers a magnificent view over the bay.

Rejoining the main road, you proceed on above **Soudha,** the port for **Khania,** and now a bustling international naval station. In another 10 km. you are driving into the center of Khania.

KHANIA

With about 55,000 inhabitants, **Khania** is Crete's second

"Sintrivani"

Hania

-largest city, the capital of its own Nome, and the commercial center for all of western Crete. But what appeals to foreigners is what **Khania** is not: it is not the home of a world-famous archaeological site nor is it the focal point of hundreds of thousands of tourists. Thus, it has escaped much of the "progress" that has so transformed **Iraklion.** And not only the developments of the most recent decades. Khania was left relatively untouched throughout this century, so that a fair amount of its Venetian and Turkish heritage remains. (Even more of the Venetian old city would remain had it not been heavily bombed during **World War II.)**

Khania offers all the facilities that most travelers would require-a selection of hotels and restaurants, shops selling all kinds of items, travel agencies to make arrangements, of all kinds, a bus terminal with connections to all the villages of Khania Nome (as well as to Rethymnon and Iraklion), and everything else from a hospital to tennis courts. But it also has something Iraklion does not: its old Venetian harbor, with enough of the old buildings having survived that it has been declared a Greek national landmark. This means that the facades around the harbor cannot be changed-but it does not mean that someone can't open another bar or discotheque in an old **Venetian warehouse.** Still, strolling or sitting around **Khania's harbor** is one of the true pleasures of a stay on Crete.

Until the 1960s, it could be said that nothing survived of the **Minoan** settlement reputed to have been in this area. Then it was discovered, right where it should have been: on the very site chosen by the Venetians as the ideal place to base a city. Excavations have not yet turned up anything that spectacular (although some items of importance to scholars, such as Linear A tablets: see p. 19), but some of the delay is due to the fact that the Venetian and modern city sits on top of the **Minoan** structures. Known to **Homer** and the ancient **Greeks** as **Kydonia,** the city was prominent in the **Hellenistic** and **Roman** periods, but it seemed to fade during the **Byzantine era.** The **Venetians,** however, chose to make it into a city that would rival **Candia (Iraklion).** They called it **La Canea** and built a great wall around it during the 16th century; only along the west side has enough survived to give some impression of its ambitions.

Within this walled city the Venetians built countless churches, public buildings, homes, gateways, and harbor installations. Some of the latter-arsenals, like those in Iraklion (p. 35)-are still to be seen along the edge of the commercial port. Up on the high ground-which is where the Minoan remains may be seen, also- is the **Venetian Archive** and the arcade of **St. Mark.** Churches and various architectural fragments can be seen as you stroll around the old quarters. As for the **Turks,** they took over many of the Venetian structures, as usual, and in the case of some churches, simply added minarets to make them mosques. But the **Mosque** of **Djamissia,** or of **Hassan Pacha,** was erected on the side of the harbor, and its domes still provide an exotic touch (if the restaurant and information office now there somewhat detract from exoticism). Again, the best way to get a sense of the Turkish presence is to walk the back streets.

The most impressive **Venetian church** to have survived is **San Francesco,** for many years now serving as the **Archaeological Museum** for finds from Khania Nome. From **Neolithic** through **Minoan, early Greek, classical Greek, Hellenistic,** and **Roman times,** the finds are not individually dramatic, but the collection as a whole provides a sense of how fine even the most modest work could be in a corner of the ancient world.

Khania also has a **Historical Museum,** strong1 on displays relating to Crete's struggle against the Turks. It also has a lot of materials relating to **Eleftherios Venizelos,** as he was born near **Khania (Mournies)** and based his campaign for Crete's indepedence here. (Thus it is that he is buried outside Khania: see p. 90). There is a **Naval Museum,** too, with some displays of historical interest-and it is in the courtyard behind the museum that plays are sometimes given in the summer. Other than these museums, you do best to walk around on your own in Khania. To the east of the old town is the **Khalepa Quarter,** largely the product of the early years of this century, when **Prince George** selected it as his residence and capital, so that anyone with ambitions settled here: some of the homes are quite exuberant. This Prince George, by the way, was

Khania: A typical street of the Old City

simply a younger son of the then **King of Greece** (and as such, a **Dane**, not a Greek!), and although he did his best to serve as an impartial administrator, he could not resist the tide of history - nor **Venizelos** - and he had to leave after the uprising of 1905. His old administrative headquarters now houses the courts of this district. And somewhat further out on the edge of this quarter is the house of **Venizelos,** while in the garden opposite is the **Russian-style Orthodox Church** of Mary Magdalene, the gift of Prince George's mother.

EXCURSIONS FROM KHANIA
THE AKROTIRI

Anyone who spends more than a day or so in **Khania** will want to take at least a few hours and drive out to the **Akrotiri**-"the promontory"

that bulges out from Khania and helps to form **Soudha Bay.** (It also is the location of **Khania's airport.**) Even those with no previous knowledge of **Venizelos** and modern Cretan history have by now gained some awareness of the special role this man has for modern Cretans, and his monumental tombsite confirms this: only some 7 km. out of Khania up on the hill overlooking the city, the tombs (for his son, **Sophocles,** a lesser Greek politician, is also buried here) create their own sense of homage while providing a magnificent view of Khania. And this site was not selected by chance: it was here in 1897 that some Cretans raised the Greek flag in defiance of the **Great Powers** (who were still trying to placate the **Ottoman Turks**); when the Great Powers' ships fired on them, so the story goes, one Cretan stood up and held the flag in his hands (while the sailors of the fleet cheered his heroism!).

For a pleasant ride: Khania

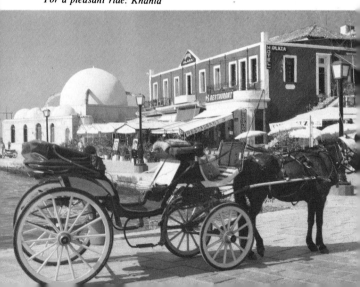

Foreigners who come to Crete expecting to see the **Minoans** revered must understand, from such tales and locales and heroes, that the more recent struggles for union with **Greece** occupy a larger place in the hearts of modern Cretans.

Another 10 km. out toward the north-central part of the Akrotiri is the **Monastery of Ayia Triadha,** built in the first half of the 17th century with the support of a converted Venetian, **Zangarola,** and thus showing (like **Arkadhi:** p. 24) a strong **Italianate** influence in its architecture. A still further drive to the north would lead to **Gouverneto Monastery,** dedicated to a local hermit-saint, **John,** who lived in the nearby **Cave of Katholiko.** To reach that and its long abandoned monastery (and **Gouverneto** is also abandoned) requires an ambitious hour's walk overland, but many local Cretans make the pilgrimage to these locales on the saint's day, October 7. The cave is fairly dramatic.

WESTERNMOST CRETE

Several of the places to be described could be visited in one long day's outing from **Khania,** but if you really wanted to experience them you should probably plan to overnight in either **Kastelli** on the north coast or **Palaiokhora** on the south coast. Increasing numbers of visitors are finding their way to this corner of the island - such as to **Souyia,** with its beach and simple accommodations - but most of these places have relatively few foreigners at any one time.

For the north coast, you head west from Khania (passing at some 2 km from town the large eagle on the left-the Germans' memorial to their airborne assault on Crete in **World War II,** and left here by the Cretans as their own memorial to that episode). Passing through the village of **Platanias,** with its popular beach, you may note offshore the islet of **Ayii Theodhori;** it has a cave that was used for cult worship at least by 2000 BC; more recently it was used as one of the preserves for the wild goat (p. 15). At **Maleme** (about 20 km), you pass the airport that the Germans landed their first gliders on and then used as the base to take over the island. At a curve in the road (about 23 km.) you turn off through the village of **Kolymvarion** and just beyond the village is the **Monastery of Ghonia,** also known as **Odhiyitrias.** It has gone through a series of reconstructions since the 17th century, but it has some interesting architectural

German military Cemetery in Maleme

Belltower in Castelli Kissamou   *Monastery of Ghonia (Odhiyitria)*

details and some ikons of value. Some meters down the road a modern building is an **Academy** maintained by the Orthodox Church to host church conferences, particularly those furthering the international ecumenical movement. (Yet another unexpected encounter on a remote shore of Crete.)

Continuing on along the main road west, you arrive (at 43 km.) at **Kastelli-Kissamou** (the last name, its district, to distinguish it from other **Kastellis** on the island.) A port since the days of the pre-classical Greeks, it has recently yielded some **Roman remains,** including a mosaic (since covered over to protect it). The **Venetians** treated it as a fairly important town (one **Venetian church** and remnants of the walls survive) but **Kastelli** has never entered the mainstream. Today, at least, it is a stop on a ship that plies between **Piraeus** and the **Peloponnesos** and **Kythera,** so it has some chance of attracting visitors. (It does have several hotels.)

On the Waterfront: Khania

Most people will pass through, though, and head for one of the two major attractions of the western coast. One is **Phalasarna,** up at the base of the westernmost peninsula that extends north from Crete. Phalasarna probably served as a port for inland settlements from pre-classical times on, but the sparse remains are from the **Hellenistic** and **Roman periods.** (The so-called throne is probably a sarcophagus standing on its end.) What makes Phalasarna of some interest - besides the dramatic view and the sense of being at the end of Crete, is the fact that the island has risen so during the centuries since Phalasarna served as a port that its harbor works are now many meters removed from the sea. Other sites around Crete - some upraised from earlier sea levels and some sunken, This nun-confirm that Crete has undergone considerable shifting over the millenniums. Off this peninsula's northern tip, by the way, is the islet of **Gramvousa** with a **Venetian fort** and other structures; you would have to arrange for a local boat to take you out.

A more appealing trip would be down the west coast to the **Convent of Khrysoskalitisia.** In fact, the best road down is via **Kaloudiana,** a village just off the main east-west road some 2 km. east of Kastelli (that is, heading toward Khania). By either route, the distances aren't that great, but the driving is slow (and the vistas rewarding). This nunnery, now all but deserted, crowns a rocky prominence near the southwest corner of the island. (One story claims that its name, "golden stairs", refers to the stairs to the convent that reveal themselves as golden except to anyone who has lied.) And another few kilometers (but a rough road!) south of the convent is the almost tropical lagoon of **Elaphanosi** and its offshore islet. Here, at least, you **may** be alone on Crete.

The southern coast of this 93

part of Crete is best approached by taking the turn south off the main east-west road, at **Tavronitis** (some 20 km. west of Khania, some 23 km. east of Kastelli). The drive itself is half the point of the trip. The town at the end, **Palaiokhora**, is nothing special, although some people enjoy staying in such end-of-the-line ports. There are also boats from here to some of the other small ports along the south coast of Crete as well as to the island of **Gavdhos,** some 50 km. offshore-and thus probably the southernmost land of Europe. (There have been two boats a week.) It has been claimed that this was **Calypso's** isle, but this is hard to support; however, it is mentioned in the **Bible** (Acts XXVII:16) as **Clauda,** which **Paul** passed by. Today only a few people live there to tend their sheep.

Of course all over this part of Crete are the countless churches with frescoes, the many minor archaeological sites, the villages and locales with their historical associations and contemporary charms. But the one remaining destination of general interest is the **Gorge** of **Samaria.**

THE GORGE OF SAMARIA

For increasing numbers of visitors to Crete, this excursion has become the highlight of their time on the island. Not too many years ago, the people who annually made the passage through the gorge could be counted in the hundreds. Now thousands go through-in one day!

Exactly what is this phenomenon that attracts so many people? The **Samaria Gorge** is a natural gorge, formed over millions of years by upheavals of the land and the wearing-down effects of water. The whole passage involves an 18 km. walk, although the gorge in the strict sense is only about half that distance. It varies from 40 meters to 3 meters, and the sheer sides rise from 300 to 600 meters up. There are several endemic wild-flowers, and many unusual birds to be seen. The wild goat that once thrived here was all but wiped out until the government preserved the species on offshore islets (p. 16); now the goats have been re-introduced back-but you are not likely to see any. In 1962, the Greek government declared this area to be the **White Mountains National Park** in order to protect its wildlife and other distinctive features. Its name, by the way, comes from **Ossia Maria,** a saint who gave her name to a chapel at the one village that used to be at about the midpoint through the passage; her name, in turn, became corrupted into "**Samaria**". (She is not the mother of *Christ,* either, but an early **Christian martyr** from Egypt.)

The walk can be made in about 5-6 hours by most people-starting, that is, from the entrance at the edge of the **Omalos Plain.** You do not need any special gear, although comfortable and sturdy shoes are appreciated. There is fresh spring water and running stream water most of the way, but you might like to bring your own snacks. At the end, along the coast, there are tavernas serving simple meals and refreshments.

Samaria Gorge

When to go? You cannot go much before mid-April nor after mid-November because of the water level in the gorge. Also, because there is not that much traffic outside the main season, you would have a much harder time getting to the start (by bus) and away from the end (by boat). Obviously, the earlier or later in the season you can make your passage, the fewer people. During the main season, avoid the weekends if possible, but if you do find yourself going through on a busy day, relax and enjoy the occasion as a sort of moving festival of nations. Many Cretans, of all ages, now go through, too, so you don't have to feel it's only a tourists' treat.

How to get there? Although the passage can be reversed (that is, you can come in at the south shore and make your way up to the Omalos), most everyone does it from the Omalos on down. The problem, in case it's not clear, is that when you come out at the

A small church in Ayia Roumeli

coast at **Ayia Roumeli,** there are no roads; you must take a boat to a town along the coast; again, for most people, this means east to **Khora Sfakion** (and for a few, west to **Palaiokhora**). It then follows that whatever vehicle brought you to the top of the gorge, some 42 km. from Khania, will be of no use to you unless someone else is staying behind to drive it (either all the way up and around down to **Khora Sfakion,** or back to Khania). That is why most people take either the public bus or a tour bus to the **Omalos.** (Taxis are another possibility for a group with more money than time.) Then, after your boat ride to Khora Sfakion, you get either another public bus or the same tour bus back to Khania. And this may be one of those occasions where a tour bus is well worth the extra charge: it guarantees you a seat when it leaves from Khania (an at early hour) and it guarantees you a seat from Khora Sfakion when you are probably in no condition to fight the crowds in a public bus.

As for the passage itself, it should not – and can not – be described in guidebook prose. You start at the edge of the **Omalos Plain** at about 1200 meters above sea level and descend down the rather steep **Xyloskalon** ("wooden stairs"). After some 2 km. the descent becomes more gentle and you pass alongside the cool little chapel of **Ayios Nikolaos.** The foot trail passes above the stream until you arrive at Samaria, the village that gave the gorge its name and now is deserted-although there is a phone and first aid station here for emergencies. Many people like to picnic at this

Khora Sphakion

point. Proceeding on, you soon must make your way along and across the stream; there are over 20 fords, now neatly and solidly arranged. Eventually you pass through the narrowest and most dramatic section of the gorge, and soon come out at the wide rocky river delta above the coast. You pass the church of **Our Lady of Roumeli,** and then the old village of **Ayia Roumeli** and make your way to the shore where a new settlement has grown up to serve the thousands of people who gather here to await the boats. The boats come in from **Khora Sfakion** starting mid-afternoon, and somehow every one gets away.

It's about a 1 1/2 hour boat ride to Khora Sfakion, plenty of time to collect your breath and thoughts. Most people now race for a bus and head directly back to Khania, but Khora Sfakion has overnight accommodations and could be an interesting place to spend a night if you have the time. During the 16th century, Khora Sfakion was said to number 3,000 people and 100 churches. More important than its numbers was its role as capital of a region of Crete, Sfakia, that never really succumbed to the various foreign occupiers of the island (nor, some would say, to their own fellow Cretan and Greek authorities). The **Sfakians** had a reputation for being a law unto themselves- whether as smugglers, sheepstealers, resistance fighters, or just plain settlers of their own feuds. Now that is pretty much a life of the past, and most foreigners will not see **Sfakia** as different from the rest of Crete.

About 12 km. to the east of Khora Sfakion, right along the shore, sits **Frangokastello,** an ambitious fort erected by the **Venetians** during the 14th century. In 1828, many **Sfakians** died while defending the fort against the **Turks,** and Cretans say that their ghosts may be seen riding along the beach early in May-the **droussoulites,** or "dew shades", that may be some combination of weather and optical illusion. If you cannot be here for this occasion, at least enjoy a swim and a meal at the beach.

All over this part of Crete, of course, there are many churches and villages. The boat between Ayia Roumeli and Khora Sfakion puts in at **Loutro,** just east of the latter; this is beginning to attract 97

Market-place in Khania

people who want to avoid the "crowds" in Khora Sfakion!

On the road back to Khania, you pass (in about 20 km.) the fine **Plain of Askiphou,** with its old **Venetian fort** atop a little hill. Another 20 km. and you arrive at Vrises, rejoining the old east-west road, and arrive (in another 32 km.) at **Khania.** A day that started about 5:30 AM will probably be ending around 9 PM, but it seems worth it to all who have made the passage.

And it is a fitting climax to a visit to Crete. For whatever you come to this island to see or seek, you usually end up being moved by the natural landscape and phenomena.

3. Everyday Pleasures
SHOPPING FOR SOUVENIRS

Most visitors to Crete will want to take home some locally made object as a memento of this special place, and there is no shortage of shops catering to that desire. What may prove more difficult is to find something truly indigenous, as there has been such a proliferation of mass produced and standardized "**Greek souvenirs**". As for something truly old-a genuine work of folk art, say, such as a piece of embroidery or an authentic piece of old jewelry-this is out of the question for most people. There is simply not that much any longer made available on the market. Claims may be made in certain shops that such-and-such an item is very old and unique, but one would have to possess

Herb Seller in Rethymnon

great expertise to be certain. The best attitude is simply to look for what one likes and can afford and not become overly concerned with its age. And that leaves a lot of different objects to choose from.

Ceramics: The shops are overflowing with all kinds of ceramicware. Some of it is in a neo-Greek style that has little or nothing to do with Crete or its traditions. But there are many fine reproductions of **Minoan vases**-the very vases that one can see in the **Iraklion Museum.** And they at least are handpainted by modern artisans. Meanwhile, there has emerged in recent years a number of modern ceramicists on Crete-several of them based in **Khania,** some at least displaying in **Ayios Niklaos:** the best of them adapt traditional **Minoan** and **Cretan** motifs and put them on contemporary and often functional (coffee cups, tea sets, etc) forms.

There remains one other possibility for those who are

especially interested in ceramics. In two villages of Crete-**Thrapsano,** in the **Pedhiadhas** district southeast of **Iraklion,** and **Margarites,** southeast of **Rethymnon**-the age-old methods and forms of pottery-making are practiced, including the large urns known in archaeology as **pithoi.** Visitors are welcomed by the artisans but you should inquire at a nearby **National Tourist** office before setting off specifically to observe.

Textiles: There is a tremendous variety of textiles to be seen in the shops. Some are little more than factory-produced clothing with **Cretan motifs**-racks of dresses, shirts, etc. There are also the now universal Greek shoulder bags, but Crete has a distinctive variety, one with draw cords that bunch the bag closed when it is slung over the shoulder. Occasionally you might come across some relatively older woolen blankets or "throws" or odd pieces of material. Cretan women still 99 do a lot of fine embroidery and needlework, and much of it ends up in stores as place-settings and such. There are also the white knitted sweaters, but with all respect for the work that has gone into them they are not as well-made nor nearly as long-lasting as their Irish counterparts.

Leatherwork: There is a fair selection here, including a distinctive braided belt, sandals and boots (**Khania** is the place for getting these custom-made), and shoulder bags and purses of various sizes.

Jewelry: There has been a virtual flood of jewelry through all the cities and tourist centers of Crete. The best of it may be solid quality, but it is at least as expensive as any place in the world and it is not really a local product. Some of it is Cretan-inspired, however-often drawing on **Minoan** works. There are outright imitations of antique and ancient jewelry in less-than-precious metals and stones and these are at least of souvenir value. With luck you might even find a relatively old heirloom piece.

Metalwork: Iraklion prides itself on its **metal knives** – but the handles are now usually synthetic. Also to be seen around Crete are the smallish

Khania

metal (now usually coated tin) tamata, simulacra with an image of some part of the human body that a petitioner wants to offer to a saint to request or thank for a cure. Some also have such objects as houses or cars that the petitioner wants blessed.

There remain still other items that you might consider. There is the molded breadrings-floral and other motifs are molded around the top crust and after baking they are covered with a kind of shellac for preserving as a souvenir. Don't overlook the **Cretan dittany**, other herbs, and herbtea. Too large for most people are the hand-carved chairs. And just by keeping your eyes open while walking by the most unpromising shops you may see some object that appeals as a memento of your Cretan visit.

EATING
AND
DRINKING

There is no denying that one of the pleasures of travelling on a place such as Crete is to partake of the special foods and drinks. If nothing else, eating and drinking are a necessity, so they might as well be done with a little knowledge and imagination so that the routine is converted into yet another point of contact with what is distinctively Cretan.

It must also be admitted that the basic menu of Crete is that to be found throughout most of Creece today. (See FOOD and DRINK under Practical Information A to Z.) But there are enough little variations and specialties on Crete to make the experience at least occasionally different. Most of the main ingredients and main courses will be fairly standard-although some people claim to find Cretan chicken and pork especially tasty. Crete's seafoods are as good as any place in Greece, but nothing that different. In **Iraklion** they are fond of **giovarlakia,** meatballs in an egg-lemon sauce, and in **Khania** there is **chochlioi,** snails with potatoes.

The vegetables of Crete don't differ that much, although again, some will claim that the Cretan tomatoes and cucumbers, in full season, are unbeatable. Cretans suck on raw artichoke leaves as an hors d'oeuvre, and they make a tasty little spinach pie. But it is the Cretan fruits that excel. Many places in Greece claim their oranges are the best, but Crete yields to no one. Watermelons on Crete seem especially juicy and tasty, and there are a few weeks in June when the local strawberries are delicious. Crete's bananas aren't anything that special, but there are other fruits-cherries,

apricots, peaches, plums. And try the pomegranates and fresh figs. And of course the table grapes during the brief harvest season.

Crete doesn't really have any distinctive desserts but there is a tasty **bougatsa** (cheese or custard in a flaky pastry) to be found in **Iraklion** and **Khania**. They also make **loukoumadhes**, doughnut-like and covered in honey. More appealing to some people will be the Cretan cheeses made from goat's milk-the **mizithra, manouri, graviera,** and **anthotiro**-all a change from the better-known **feta**. Perhaps best of all is the fresh yoghurt of Crete.

And then there are the drinks of Crete. Cretans are actually proud of their water and there is nothing quite like a glass from a cold mountain spring. There are some decent wines of **Crete-Minos, Gortinos, Phaestos, Brousko** and **Kissamos** are brand-varieties. Cretans favor a stronger version of the familiar ouzo, known as **raki** or **tsipouro;** still stronger and distinctively **Cretan** is **mournoraki,** a mulberry-based liqueur from **Rethymnon.** There is also the **soumadha** from the **Neapolis** region: almonds are crushed to produce a milky liquid that is then flavored with orange-blossom water; this is then diluted with hot water in the winter or cold water in the summer to give a slightly sweetish refresher. And try the various Cretan herb teas.

Raki (tsikoudhia) distiller

ACTIVITIES
AND
DIVERSIONS

Just as Crete offers far more than **Minoan sites** and sunny beaches, Crete can be more than a place for a passive vacation. Crete offers much to those who like to do more than just look on or lounge about while on their vacation.

SPORTS
AND OUTDOOR
ACTIVITIES

To those whose idea of a holiday is to remain or become athletically active, Crete offers a variety of possibilities. To begin, look under the following listings in **Practical Information A to Z** for general remarks about these subjects, all of which apply to Crete: **Sports, Swimming, Mountaineering, Tennis, Underwater Sports, Yachting, Fishing, Hunting.** Here are certain aspects that apply more especially to Crete.

Swimming and Watersports: On the edges of Iraklion, Khania, and **Rethymnon** there is at least one beach open to the public with changing facilities and places to at least snack. Many Cretan beaches now have vendors renting paddleboats and sail-surfboards. Waterskiing is offered by several of the major beach resorts, and it has been customary for the operators to rent the boat (and their services) if no one from the resort needs them at that moment. As for snorkeling, Crete may not

Sitia

offer the spectacular underwater experiences of tropical islands, but there are certainly some interesting things to see along the coasts.

Fishing and Hunting: There is no freshwater fishing on Crete, but everyone likes to drop a line in the harbors and you could also rent a small boat and fish offshore. Some Cretan men do like to hunt small game-rabbits and birds-but most visitors won't get the opportunity to do this. One special kind of hunting, however, has been arranged for very special foreigners. In order to save the wild goat of Crete from extinction, many were brought to breed on three small islands off the north coast of Crete. On **Dia,** just off **Iraklion,** the population so expanded that in recent years the government has allowed people to hunt the goat there. There are strict limits on the type of weapon and ammunition-and the license, fees for any killed, and transportation make it a rich man's sport at best. Considering that the goats can't get too far away, it's questionable whether it's even a true sport.

On the beach

Mountaineering: Crete offers some fine opportunities for those who like to climb or even just to walk the trails of mountains. There are hardly any world-class peaks (see p. 13), but no one should underestimate the challenges. Not only should you be properly equipped-proper-clothing shoes, water, and food-you should at least have a map and compass. Indeed, unless you are truly experienced you should have a local guide. And don't be mislead by weather conditions down on the plains. The **Greek Mountaineering Club** has branch offices in **Iraklion** and **Khania,** and the **National Tourist offices** can put you in touch with them. And for those who aren't quite up to taking on a mountain, there is the famed **Samaria Gorge,** a day's excursion that is described in some detail on p. 13

Caves: As mentioned elsewhere (p. 13), Crete has over half the known caves of Greece. Many of them are rich in their mythological, legendary, and historical associations (and are described in the section on excursions). All the caves of Crete so far have been left natural-that is, they have not been wired for electricity-but several are now kept locked and admission is only at set times: the local Tourist Information office should be able to inform you of the current schedule. Even more experienced spelunkers should contact the local authorities before undertaking any explorations.

Sunset

Vai: Eastern Crete

FESTIVALS

The general remarks about **Holidays** (in Practical Information A to z) should be underscored when it comes to Crete: perhaps no place in Greece observes its festivals quite so intensely. Beyond the major national holidays–Easter, May 1, Assumption of the Virgin (August 15)–there are countless special festivals around Crete, many of them associated with saints' namedays. Anyone interested should start by asking at the local Tourist Information office; with luck you'll run into someone who is going to celebrate a nameday or a baptism or a wedding in a village and you may get asked along. There will usually be a church service, lots or eating and drinking, and some music and dancing. In addition to these traditional festivals, there are several more recent ones that have been introduced on Crete: Rethymnon observes a wine festival near the end of July, and on November 7-9 Rethymnon and the nearby Monastery of Arkadhi observe the explosion of 1866; Sitia has a grape festival in August; Khersonisos has a watermelon festival in July; Skine-Kydonias has an orange festival in April. And there are still more such special events. Ask around when you arrive.

PROFESSIONAL ENTERTAINMENT

In recent years both Iraklion and Khania have sponsored

Surfing

"mini-festivals" with professional actors offering plays, usually those with some special Cretan associations (such as those from the Cretan-Italian "renaissance" of the 17th century). In Iraklion, the plays are presented on the top of the Venetian fort in the harbor; in Khania, in the courtyard of the Firka bastion at the far end of the harbor. The performances are in Greek but they should still speak to anyone interested in the theater. There is not much other "high culture" on Crete. Touring musicians occasionally give recitals. Once in awhile a superior movie-and-dance groups who perform in authentic regional costumes; they are amateurs byt they have worked hard to keep up the traditional culture. They appear in public on various occasions when you see them free; on other occasions they have given public performances with paid admission. Ask when you arrive on Crete if such an event is scheduled for your time.

MUSIC & DANCE

One of the special pleasures Crete has to offer is its extraordinary heritage of music and dance. **Zorba the Greek** may have left some people with certain false impressions, but the spirit behind the music and the dance in that film is certainly Cretan. And although the radio, phonograph, and cassettes have now undeniably released a lot of foreign music into the Cretan community, even young Cretans still enjoy their traditional music and dance.

The first music that visitors to Crete will probably encounter is that blaring form the music shops in the main cities. Some of it is indeed pseudo-folk musik, but it is also true that some of Greece's best modern composers – such as Theodorakis and Hadzidakis – have drawn on traditional Greek music while creating more contemporary works. Certain tavernas and restaurants and even nightclubs feature "authentic Cretan music", and although the performers may be doing it as professionals, they may still give a fair introduction to some of the traditional music.

Occasionally a nightclub in Iraklion or Khania has actually featured a genuine Cretan folksinger, who plays the traditional instruments and sings in an authentic manner. Ask if any such is active when you're on the scene. Travel agencies, meanwhile, now offer regularly scheduled visits to several villages that work to keep some of the old ways alive: these are usually advertised as "A Cretan Night" or some such name, and involve a meal, some music and dancing by costumed locals (and the inevitable visits to souvenir shops). Not to everyone's taste, but for some the closest they may come to the real thing. Under **Professional Entertainment** (above), the folklore groups that occasionally appear in public have been described. Best of all, though, is to get invited to some village on a special holiday or for a wedding or baptism: this is where the true Cretan music and dance are to be experienced.

The main instrument used to make Cretan folk music is a lyre, or **lyra**: a rather elegant 3-stringed instrument that is held upright while it sits on the upper leg and is bowed. The Cretan **lyra** is tuned in fifths, as is the violin often used to accompany it; the lute, clarinet, and pipes are sometimes used. (The bouzouki, both as an instrument and a style of music, are not particulalry common on Crete.) The music of Greek folk songs – melodies, modes, scales, intervals, and such elements – can generally be traced back to Byzantine music, and it is in turn assumed that this Byzantine music grew out of ancient Greek music, so Cretan folk songs can be heard as at least distant reverberations of a very ancient tradition.

Whole books are required to categorize the different types of Cretan folk music, but all that need be known is that there are certain basic types. Usually, too, this folk music is sung on social occasions – weddings, baptisms, holidays – along with the eating and drinking. (It should also be said that it is almost entirely the province of men on these public occasions.) But other songs are sung on other, less public occasions: to accompany work, to soothe children, to convey love. There is one large group known as "songs of the road", sung by villagers as they move along the road to get the bride and bring her to her wedding and then to transport the dowry to the couple's new house. Still another special type of song is the **miroloyi,** or lament, in which the living are asked to confront the inevitability of death.

Then there are the **paraloyi,** or ballads: shortish, fictional narratives that focus on a crucial dramatic episode involving such themes as the abduction of a bride or avenging a family's honor or the return of a dead brother. There are also the klephtic songs, narratives in praise of the **klepthi,** those guerrilla warriors who used the moun-

Kalyves village

tains as their bases from which to fight the Turks during the centuries of occupation.

Many of these songs and themes may be found throughout Greece. But Crete has two particular types of songs. One is the **mantinadhes,** rimed couplets that are supposed to be imrpovised but which in practice draw on a great repertoire of stock formulas. **Mantinadhes** are both pungent and poignant, allusive and elusive. Men sometimes compete with each other, tossing off one and then waiting for the other singer to come up quickly with another **mantinadha** on the same theme.

Another special group of Cretan folk songs are known as **rizitika**-"songs of the roots," in reference to the "roots" of the White Mountains of western Crete, where these songs are most current. About 30 basic melodies are used for the **rizitika,** many of which have patriotic themes – especially expressing the Cretans' desire for independence from their various occupiers over the centuries. But many **rizitika** are on other themes – love songs, homesickness and exile, religious, songs of shepherds or hunters or farmers, even humorous or satirical songs. Traditionally men sing these songs while sitting around the table, often with one side singing a phrase that is then repeated by the men on the other side; often there are several melodies going at once, with no attempt at harmony.

Crete has also given birth to two of the finest examples of Greek popular poetry that are now usually sung as solo works to basic melodies. Until recently, at least, the singers were generally illiterate moun-tain men – shepherds, chesse-makers, and such – often well along in years and sometimes even blind: the tradition of Homer and the bard is clear. (Today, some younger Cretans have deliberately set about to maintain the performance tradition). One of these folk poems is an example of the heroic poem like the klephtic songs, sung to entertain but also to edify the younger generation, to pass on the tradition of hereoic **aretê,** or "excellence". This is the **Song of Daskaloyiannis.** recounting the tragic failure of the revolt of 1770 (see p. 23) and the execution of its Sfakian leader, Daskaloyiannis. Sixteen years old after the event this poem was dictated to a scribe by an illiterate cheesemaker-bard, and there are still Cretans who know all of its 1.032 lines.

Still more remarkable is that there have been Cretans who could recite most if not all of the 10,052 lines of the **Erotokritos,** Crete's other gift to postclassical Greek literature. This, however, is definitely a composed work, attributed to Vincenzo Kornaros in about 1645. It is based on a European romance, but the plot has been adapted to Cretan scenes and the diction is in a Cretan folk idiom. It is more chanted than sung, but it would be quite an experience if you could be directed to someone who sings this work.

Closely related to the folk songs are the folk dances of Crete. Again, they are related to those of the rest of Greece, and they may be categorized in different ways. There are the **syrtos,** or "trailing" type of dances, where the dancers "trail" or follow the leader. There are the **pidiktos,** or "leaping" type of dances, which involve just what the name suggests. The dances are usually accompanied by one or another stringed instrument – lute or violin or whatever – and often by clarinets. Many of the dances are somewhat the same all over Greece, but each district also has its special variants and names of the dances are often assigned by the places they are claimed to have originated or at least become most popular. Thus, on Crete there is the **khaniotikos**, from Khania, or the **sitiakos**, from Sitia. Other dances popular on Crete include the **ortzes,** the **sousta**, the **kastrinos,** and the **malevysiotikos.** In fact, you might see any of these being danced by Cretan males in city tavernas or nightclubs (even if they are doing it to impress the foreign females), but best would be to see them danced in the villages. Better still would be to learn the basic steps and join in.

For Crete welcomes and rewards the active participant in its full life.

4.   Traveling to Crete

Although there are several alternatives (all described below), for most people the decision as to how to go over to Crete comes down to a choice between flying over from Athens or taking a ship from Piraeus, the port of Athens. Ship passage is cheaper – decidedly so for Deck Class – but not if you consider you are saving on a hotel room: most of the ships depart early evening and arrive early morning. For some, that 10-12 hours is more than they want to spend and the air passage of 40-50 minutes is appealing. Traditionalists maintain that the only way to arrive on Crete is to come up on deck early in the morning and see the island's mountains coming into view. Consider taking ship there and plane back.

Especially in high tourist season, and especially for airplane passage, buy your tickets as soon in advance as possible.

AIR

Most people will be flying by one of the scheduled flights of **Olympic Airways** from **Athens** to **Iraklion** or **Khania.** Many international airlines can make connections with these **Olympic flights,** but be

A window in Khania

careful: **Olympic Airways** uses the **West Air Terminal** (for both its international and domestic flights) while all other airlines use the **East Air Terminal**. There are frequent bus connections between the two terminals, but the extra time (about 45 minutes) must be allowed for.

There are several flights daily from Athens **to Iraklion** and also to Khania (slightly fewer to Khania) and an equal number of return flights. Flight time is usually the scheduled 45 minutes. As Khania is a bit closer, the fare is slightly less. One possibility: enter Crete by one of these cities and leave from the other, planning your itinerary around this route.

During the tourist season, **Olympic** offers some flights that connect **Iraklion** and **Rhodes**. And there have been attempts at supporting service between **Iraklion** and **Santorini** during the tourist season. Inquire when you arrive in Greece about this or any other possibilities. There has also been direct service between **Iraklion** and **Cyprus (Nicosia)** at times.

There remain the many charter flights that now fly directly to Crete (usually **Iraklion**) from foreign cities (sometimes with a stop at **Athens**). These charter flights usually involve holiday "packages"-including hotels, meals, etc. Consult a travel agent.

SHIPS

Most people take a ship from **Piraeus** to one of the Cretan ports-Iraklion or **Khania** (actually the latter's port is **Soudha**, a few miles to the 112 east). Most ships depart-in

both directions-early evening and arrive 10-12 hours later in early morning. There is at least one ship daily to and from **Iraklion,** slightly fewer per week to and from **Khania.** Tickets may be purchased at the ship lines' offices in Iraklion, Khania, or Piraeus and at travel agents in various cities. There are different classes of tickets, from **Luxury** (a suite) to **Deck** (you sleep on any available chair), but most people will be interested in **Second Class** or **Tourist Class:** the main difference is that if you are travelling with a group of two or more and of different sexes, you would be split up by taking **Tourist Class.** Snacks and complete meals are available on these ships. All the ships also transport vehicles that can be driven right into the holds; fees vary according to size of the vehicle.

There is ship service between Crete and **Rhodes,** but the ports on Crete are **Ayios Nikolaos** and **Sitia**-not **Iraklion** - so this means getting to one of these eastern cities in time to make the connection. (These ships usually stop at three small islands in between - **Kassos, Karpathos,** and **Khalki.**)

There is also ship service between **Iraklion** and **Santorini** -several ships during the tourist season. These ships put in at other **Cycladic** islands en route to and from **Piraeus** and Crete-Mykonos, Naxos, and others. Inquire when in Greece about current schedules.

There has also been a ship from **Kastelli-Kissamos,** the small port to the far west of Crete to the island of **Kythera** and then on to various ports on the **Peloponnesos** while en route to **Piraeus.** The reverse

On the boat

route is also serviced, and this offers an interesting variation on getting to or from **Crete**.

Yet another possibility has been a ship that provides service from **Ancona**, the **Italian** port up on the **Adriatic Sea,** via **Patras (Greece), Crete (Iraklion)** to **Alexandria, Egypt.** Such services are apt to change, so inquire a at a travel agent. Aside from this line, it is hard to guarantee any scheduled service between Crete and foreign ports; there might be some ships-from **France, Italy, Yougoslavia, Cyprus, Israel, Turkey** - but you must inquire carefully at a travel agent.

A major alternative for many are the cruise ships that regularly put in at Crete - usually departing from **Piraeus** and usually stopping only at Iraklion. Of course such ships take on only those who sign on for the complete cruise and they usually make only a one-day stop at Iraklion.

Of more limited appeal are two other possibilities-charte-

red yachts or **kaikis.** The former are discussed at **Yachting** in **Practical Information A to Z. Kaikis** are the small boats used for a variety of chores by local sailors; usually they confine themselves to one island, and they're not really in the business of transporting tourists, but you might find one that could take you for an agreed-upon fee from one port to another.

5. Traveling around Crete

There are no airplane flights connecting Cretan cities-nor, if it isn't known, are there any railways on Crete. As for ships between **Cretan ports**, there are the above-described **kaikis-** but these are not reliable. There are no ships connecting the main cities along the northern coast, but there are small ships connecting some of the southern ports-**Khora Sfakion** and **Ayia Roumeli** (at the end of the **Samaria Gorge**), with a stop at **Loutro**; a ship to **Gavdhos Island** from **Palaiokhora**; another from **Ierapetra** to **Gaidhouronissi islet,** off the southeast coast. But for most visitors to Crete, other means of transportation are utilized.

BUS

There is public bus service not only connecting all the main cities but also from these cities to virtually all the villages and sites that most people will want to visit. One possible inconvenience is that the schedules between the main cities and the villages have been set up to allow the villagers to come into the city early in the morning and return home late afternoon-

Fishing

the reverse of most tourists' schedules. Winter and summer schedules vary insignificantly as far as most tourists are concerned. Fares are relatively cheap. Tickets may usually be obtained just before departure, but especially during the tourist season you are advised to buy yours at the bus terminal sometime in advance; seats are reserved (although in practice people often ignore the exact number) and standees limited. (Save all bus tickets in case an inspector comes through.) Many visitors still find the public buses the best introduction to Crete.

There are also the many tour buses now operated by various travel agencies. These take groups to specific sites or locales and require purchasing a ticket sometime in advance. The rates usually include a guide who provides an account of the trip and the place visited. The buses are quite comfortable (and are often called **"Pullmans"**); for many people, these tour buses offer a fine alternative to get to several less accessible places.

CAR

If you bring your own car over to Crete, you will certainly be able to cover far more of the island in a shorter time than if you rely on public transportation. Most of the roads are in fine to adequate condition, but some are becoming rough and filled with unexpected holes; if you like to get to every remote site, you must be prepared to drive down some fairly rough dirt roads, but they can all be managed. Gasoline (petrol) of all grades is available all over the island, although you should probably try to keep as full a tank as possible before going off to remote points.

Distances on Crete are never that long, but curves and climbs add to the time required. (For more about **Driving**, see that entry at **Practical Information A to Z**).

Yet another possibility is to rent (hire) a car from one of the many agencies based in **Iraklion, Khania, Rethymnon,** or **Ayios Nikolaos.** The large international agencies-Hertz, Avis, etc.-are all over Crete and there are many local firms. Rates are generally fixed by law, and if the international agencies charge a bit more they offer several advantages such as pick-up and drop-off at airports or providing quick replacement vehicles in case of an accident. (For more about **Car Rental,** see that entry at **Practical Information A to Z.**)

TAXI

Another possibility is to hire a taxi to take you direct to some site or locale. Taxis are relatively cheap and if you use public buses for the long trips and a taxi for the short final distances you might arrive at the best compromise between time and cost. There is usually at least one taxi available in all except the smaller villages of Crete (as Cretans themselves rely on taxis). (For more about **Taxis,** see that entry at **Practical Information A to Z.**)

MOTORBIKE, SCOOTER, BICYCLE RENTAL

In a few main cities and centers of tourism on Crete it is now possible to rent various types of motorbikes, motor scooters, or bicycles. (For more on **Bicycles** or **Motorbikes.**

Balli beach

6.   When to go

Assuming you have some choice in exactly when you are to visit Crete, there are two main factors to consider (and obviously related ones)-the weather and the touristic

IRAKLION'S WEATHER			
Months	Average Air Temperature Centigrade	Average Water Temperature Centigrade	Average Rainfall millimeters
January	12°	16°	94
February	12°	16°	76
March	14°	17°	41
April	17°	18°	23
May	20°	20°	18
June	23°	23°	3
July	26°	24°	0
August	26°	25°	3
September	24°	24°	18
October	21°	23°	43
November	17°	19°	69
December	14°	17°	102

facilities.

Considering that Crete boasts of some 300 rain-free days each year, rain is not much of an issue as far as most touristis are concerned. Only 20 inches per year falls in **Iraklion,** and most of that in December, January, and February. Indeed, virtually no rain falls in June, July, August, and September (and very little in April and May) in those places where most foreigners are apt to be. It should be kept in mind, though, that when you leave the coastal areas there is appreciably more rain; and snow falls in the mountains and can actually isolate certain more remote villages. But even though the winters are relati-

Ayios Nicholaos

vely mild, most foreigners will not choose to visit Crete during those months.

If you have complete freedom of choice, the ideal months for travelling on Crete are probably May or October: these months offer the best mixture of weather and touristic amenities. April and November are also possibilities, although the weather is a bit of a risk. September has become a popular month. June, July, and August remain the busy months-and the hot months. But the occasional offshore breezes and generally cooling evenings help to alleviate the extreme heat. Visitors are strongly advised, though, to limit their outings during the heat of the day.

The other factor obviously relates to the weather. During the warmer months, when most people come to Crete, there is much more life on the island-more hotels, more restaurants, more amenities of all kinds. There are more boats and more planes. There are even several special events-plays and dance performances, for instance. A general holiday mood prevails. At the same time, some prices increase-hotels in particular. Many facilities become overcrowded: the **Samaria Gorge** may attract as many as 2,000 people on certain days during the high season. Yet no one ever goes hungry or without a bed. And those who truly dislike crowds can usually avoid them by leaving the main tourist attractions.

It comes down to personal preferences. Beware, though, of travel promotion that suggests you can enjoy water sports throughout the Cretan winter.

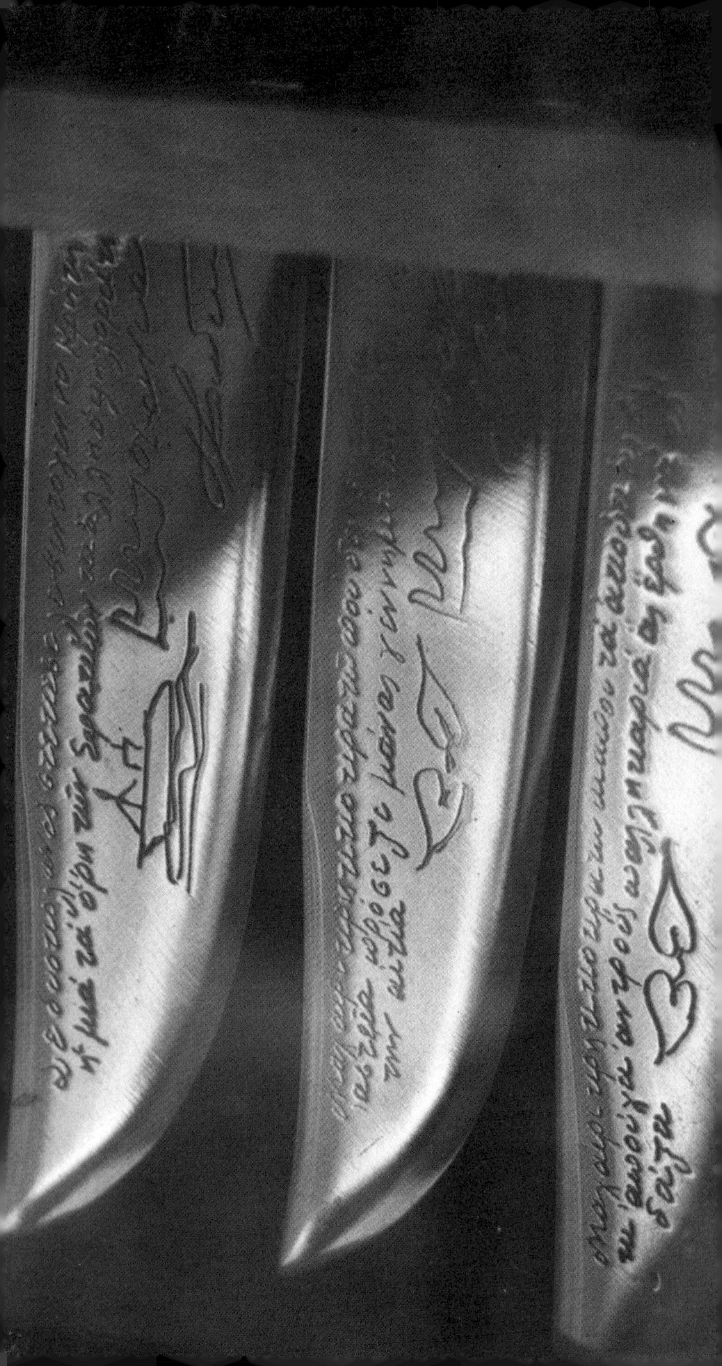

7. General Practical Information from A to Z

AIR TRAVEL

Within Greece, this is a monopoly of **Olympic Airways,** the national airline. **Olympic** has an excellent safety record. Almost all its flights originate in **Athens,** but there are some connecting routes (such as **Rhodes** and Crete in the tourist season). **Olympic** services all the major and more remote cities and islands of Greece with a variety of aircraft. During the tourist season, tremendous demands are placed on the service by the great numbers of foreigners, so you are advised to make reservations as far in advance as possible. You must be prepared for seasonal changes in schedules, too; and travel agents abroad will not always be up to date, so check your flights immediately upon arriving in Greece. Passengers who initiate their flights within Greece may be limited to 15 kilos of luggage free of charge; those connecting with flights from abroad are allowed the international limits.

All Olympic flights, both international and domestic, operate out of the **West Air Terminal of Athens' Hellinikon Airport**; all other airlines use the **East Air Terminal.** The two are connected by frequent bus service, but about 45 minutes must be allowed to move from one to the other. Olympic also provides bus service from all its airports for a modest fee, but some people may find the wait not worth the money; especially if you are with a small group, a taxi can be relatively cheap. In **Athens** itself, the intown terminal for buses to and from the airport its too far from the center to walk there with luggage, but it is still considerably cheaper to take a taxi to this terminal and then the bus to the airport.

ALPHABET: See GREEK LANGUAGE

ANTIQUITIES: Greece enforces a very strict law against exporting antiques and antiquities. Anything dating from before 1830 is technically an antique and cannot be exported without official permission. This might be hard to prove in the case of a piece of textile or old jewelry, but the authorities are really interested in stopping the export of such items as ikons or manuscripts. As for genuine antiquities, small items are sold by several legitimate dealers, but permission for export must be obtained: the dealers should be able to direct you to the proper government office (which has traditionally been at the **National Archaeological Service, Leoforos Vassilissis Sofias 22, Athens**). Be wary of buying anything "under the counter": if it's not genuine, you're being cheated, and if it is genuine you're apt to find yourself in trouble.

AUTOMOBILE CLUB: Greece has a privately supported automobile club or association with offices in all main cities. Its Greek name forms the acronym **ELPA,** by which it is known; it means **Hellenic**

Knives for souvenirs   119

Touring and Automobile Club. Its head office is in **Athens** at the **Pyrgos Athinon** (corner of **Vassilissis Sofias** and **Mesogeion Ave**). It can assist you in obtaining an **International Driver's license** (so long as you have a valid license-which in practice is often accepted) or provide advice about insurance or other matters. For its members, **ELPA** provides a range of services, and its emergency repair vehicles will usually stop for any vehicle along the highway.

BABYSITTERS: Greeks have traditionally relied on their "extended families" to perform babysitting, but in recent years-due primarily to the needs of foreigners-Greek women have taken up this chore for money. They are not especially cheap, relative to wages in Greece and elsewhere, but they perform a necessary service. If you need a babysitter, contact the hotel reception desk, the **Tourist Police,** a travel agency, or the **National Tourist Information office.** The higher grade hotels should almost certainly be able to provide someone.

BANKS: There is no shortage of banks in Greek cities. Their normal hours are 8 AM to 2 PM, Monday through Friday, and some open for at least foreign exchange on Saturday mornings, Sunday morning and late afternoon or early evening. But banks do close on the main Greek holidays (See HOLIDAYS), so make sure you do not leave vital transactions to those days. Most goodsized banks maintain separate counters or windows for foreign exchange so be sure you get in the right line. Banks officially-and generally in practice do-give the best exchange rate (and usually give a slightly better rate for travelers' checks than for foreign currency). If you have bought too many Drachmas and want to buy back your own currency, you must provide the receipts of the Drachma purchases, and even so you will be limited as to how much you can convert back. You may be asked for your passport in any bank transactions, so have it with you. See also MONEY.

BARBERS: There are plenty of barbers in Greece, and you shouldn't need much language to get what you want. It is customary to tip the barber about 10%; if he uses a boy for cleaning up, you give him a few extra Drachma. See also HAIRDRESSERS.

BATHING: See SWIMMING

BICYCLES FOR RENT: Bicycles may be rented-usually from renters of motorbikes, motorscooters, etc.-in the main cities and resort centers. Rates vary, but they obviously become cheaper over longer periods. And if you are planning on renting for a specific trip on a specific occasion, reserve in advance, especially during the main tourist season. See also MOTORBIKES FOR RENT

BUS TRAVEL: There is frequent public bus service both within all large Greek cities and connecting main cities to smaller villages. In the cities, you pay as you get on the bus at the rear; keep your receipt for possible inspection. For intercity travel, you usually buy the ticket at the starting point; the ticket may include a numbered seat-but Greeks often pay little attention to this. However, especially during the main tourist season, buses can quickly become crowded, so you are advised to buy your ticket as soon as possible. Schedules between main cities and outlying villages have usually been set up for the convenience of villagers who need to come into the city early in the morning and return home late afternoon, so tourists may have to plan around such schedules. If you want to get a bus at a stop along its route, be sure that you signal clearly to the approaching driver, who may not otherwise stop.

CAMPING: Officially there is no longer camping in Greece except at the locales set aside either for government or commercial campsites. The **National Tourist Organization** has a brochure listing all such places around Greece. Such campsites, like those elsewhere, offer a range of support services, from hot water to electric outlets to food. Unofficially, there is still some camping-whether in vehicles or tents-on various beaches and fields. If you do try this, at least respect the property and dispose of all your wastes in approved ways. If you didn't stay too long in one place and picked fairly remote locales, you might get away with such camping.

CAR RENTAL: There are many firms that rent cars-both the wellknown international agencies such as **Hertz** and **Avis** and many locally owned firms-in all the large cities and resort centers around Greece. Rates are generally controlled

by law, and variations are supposed to reflect different services, etc. The bigger international agencies, for example, can offer pickups and dropoffs at airports; they are also better equipped to provide quick replacement vehicles should something go wrong. Actual rates vary greatly depending on the size of vehicle, length of time, etc. You will find that it is much easier to rent a car if you have a charge card; otherwise you must leave a large deposit. You will probably want to pay the extra charge for full-coverage insurance (that is, to eliminate any problems with minor damage to the vehicle). You must produce a valid driver's license -in practice, this is accepted without the **International Driver's License.** Do volunteer the names of all individuals who may be driving the vehicle. And during the main tourist season, make your reservation as far in advance as possible.

CHARTER CRUISES: This has become a most popular way of visiting the **Greek islands.** Cruises vary from 2 days to a week or longer, and sometimes include stops at other **Mediterranean ports** (e.g. **Ephesus** or **Constantinople** in **Turkey**). They are not especially cheap, but considering that you save on hotel rooms and have to eat someplace, and that the alternatives (less comfortable small interisland ships or expensive airplanes) do not appeal to many people, these cruises become the best choice for many people. The principal disadvantage is the short time allowed on shore in most cases. Most of these cruises originate in **Athens-Piraeus,** but inquire at any travel agent for information. 121

CHURCHES: Since about 98% of all Greeks belong to the Greek Orthodox Church, it is not surprising that most churches will be of that faith. Visitors to Greece should make a point of stepping into some of these churches, whether old or new, large or small; best time is when a service is being held-even better when some special holy day or occasion such as a wedding or baptism is being celebrated. (Greeks are happy to see foreigners in attendance.) It used to be possible to step into any remote chapel, but with an increase of thefts of ikons and valuables in recent years, many chapels are now kept locked; usually the key is held by the priest or someone else in the nearest village. There are small pockets of **Roman Catholics in Greece** - in the **Ionian, Dodecannese,** and **Cycladic islands,** and of course a large foreign community in Athens - and services are held in their own churches. There are relatively few **Protestants in Greece,** and most of these are foreigners in **Athens,** where there are several **Protestant churches.** There are also Jewish synagogues in **Athens** and **Thessaloniki.**

CIGARETTES and CIGARS: Greeks continue to smoke cigarettes as though cancer had never been invented. The Greek cigarettes (and they grow a great deal of tobacco) come in all strengths and prices, and determined smokers should be able to find a brand to substitute for their otherwise very expensive favorites from home. There are limits on how many can be imported free of duty into Greece: 200 cigarettes, 50 cigars (or 200 grams of tobacco for a pipe).

CLOTHING: If you come during the hot months-May through September-you can get by in most situations with a light wardrobe. Do bring at least a sweater for cool evenings, however. And of course if you intend to spend time at higher elevations, you must bring adequate clothing-for cooler weather, possible rain, and any special requirements (such as rugged shoes for hiking). Greeks are informal dressers, and at beaches almost anything goes; however, they do not like to see people wearing beachwear in towns or in stores away from the beach; villagers are especially conservative, and you will create unnecessary comments if you parade around villages in scanty beachwear. You can always buy needed clothing in Greece, but it is not especially cheap. There are some local specialties, of course-informal shirts, shawls or sweaters, sandals, sunhats, etc.

COMPLAINTS: With literally millions of foreigners moving around Greece each year, it is impossible not to have occasional incidents or cases of dissatisfaction. Many of these arise from language problems or cultural differences. But if you feel you have a legitimate complaint, there are several possibilities. Start with the local **Tourist Police** or **National Tourist Organization office:** the emergency **phone number** for the **Tourist Police** all over Greece is **171. Athens** has a special number for handling complaints by foreigners: **135.** One way to stop possible episodes is to ask for an itemized bill or receipt that you can indicate you intend to show to the **Tourist Police.**

CONSULATES and EMBASSIES: All the major nations of the world maintain embassies in Athens, but most travelers are more apt to need help in some more remote city. Many countries maintain consulates in other Greek cities-and often in unexpected cities, due to levels of commerce or tourism in these areas. Many of these consuls are local nationals, but they are authorized to help. Likewise, even if your own country does not maintain a consulate in a particular city, another country's might be able to help if it primarily a matter-at least at the outset-of finding someone who speaks your language. (Example: You need someone to translate a Greek document.)

CREDIT CARDS: The major international and certain national credit cards are accepted in many situations around Greece. The expected scale of acceptance prevails: the more expensive and more internationally-oriented the facility (hotel, restaurant, store), the more likely they are to honor credit cards. You cannot expect small tavernas, little pensions, village shops, to honor such cards. In most cases, those places that honor credit cards display plaques or signs so indicating at the front. And in the case of car rentals, credit cards are actually preferred for they serve to assure the agencies of your credit standing. See also TRAVELERS CHECKS

CUSTOMS CONTROL: For the mass of foreigners who visit Greece, customs control is so relaxed that it will hardly be noticed. You will have to pass through passport and customs control on your first point of entry into Greece-for most people, this will mean **Athens, Piraeus,** or one of the border checkpoints at the north, or **Patras.** There are some limits, however, and although you might slip in uninspected, you should know of these. You can bring in unlimited sums of travellers checks or foreign currency, but you are limited to bringing in (and taking out) 1,500 Drachmas. Only 200 cigarettes or 50 cigars or 200 grams of tobacco can be brought in; 1 liter of liquor or 1 liter of wine may be imported. Cameras, typewriters, radios, tape-recorders may be brought in as long as they are clearly for personal use; there are some limits on weapons and you should inquire before setting out for Greece. You cannot import explosives or narcotics (or parrots!). In leaving, you are limited to how much olive oil you can take out tax-free (as well as to 1,500 Drachmas and antiques-before 1830-and antiquities without official permission: See ANTIQUITIES).

DENTISTS: Dentists are to be found in all large to middle-sized cities. Most have trained abroad (and so will speak at least one foreign language) and they will usually have quite modern equipment. Their rates should be quite reasonable. When in need of a dentist, start by asking at the hotel reception desk (especially at the better grade hotels) or the **Tourist Police:** for one thing, someone can then phone 123 ahead and explain your problem.

DOCTORS: Doctors are found in all large to middle-sized cities, although various specialists may be found only in the former. Most of these doctors will have done some of their studies abroad and so will speak at least one foreign language. Their knowledge, equipment, and techniques will be thoroughly up to date. In **Athens** especially, you must expect to pay international rates; elsewhere doctors may be somewhat cheaper. Incidentally, if you had a medical emergency in a small or remote locale, the local people would certainly help in getting a doctor to you or you to a doctor. See also PHARMACIES.

DRIVING IN GREECE: Large numbers of foreigners now drive either their own or rented vehicles around Greece. In both cases you need a **valid driver's licence,** and theoretically you should have an **International Driver's License.** It if it is your own car you are bringing into Greece, you need its registration (or log book) and you need proof of adequate insurance. There will be limits (usually about 4 months) on the length of time you can drive your car in Greece; you can usually get an extension (for 8 months) to continue driving your car without any major registration fees. The car will be entered in your passport, so if you were for any reason want to sell it in Greece, you must make very sure you are in full compliance with Greek laws governing such transactions.

Your car-and all rented vehicles - are exempt from the Greek law governing alternate Sunday regulations (even number plates-odd number plates). But foreigners must obey speed limits (and police can demand payment of fines on the spot) and you should observe parking regulations: the Greek custom is for police to remove license plates-and then force you to go around to a police station to pay the fine to get your plates back!

Fuel of all grades is available all over Greece-at some of the highest rates in the world. Because almost all Greeks drive imported cars (some foreign vehicles are now being assembled in Greece), there is no problem obtaining spare parts or experienced repairmen for your vehicle. (You may be amazed at the age of some of the boys who work on your vehicle-under adult supervision, you hope.)

Driving is on the right. Roads are not always well marked for danger spots or unusual conditions: curves, soft shoulders, fallen rocks, steep gradients-these are often not indicated. And although Greece has built up an impressive national highway system, many roads are in need of basic maintenance: it is not uncommon to encounter major potholes or rough stretches in the middle of otherwise decent highways. In addition, Greek drivers themselves retain a few habits from the days before motor vehicles were so common: they turn into main highways, stop along the road without warning, weave in and out in city streets. (Greece has one of the highest fatality rates from driving accidents.) But with basic caution, you should have no trouble driving in Greece.

124

DRUGS: Greek authorities take a very strict approach on importing drugs. On the other hand, Greek men in certain locales do smoke marijuana and use even stronger drugs. But foreigners would be advised to have nothing to do with drugs while in Greece.

DRYCLEANING: There are plenty of drycleaning establishments in all large to medium-sized cities. It is relatively cheap and fast-you should be able to get your clothing back within the day if you bring it early and make your needs clear. See also LAUNDRY.

EARTHQUAKES: Despite the publicity that attends earthquakes in Greece-from the days of **Lost Atlantis** to the ones that struck the **Athens area** in 1980 – these need not be of concern to visitors. The odds are that the most anyone will experience might be a slight tremor. One might just as well stay away from **Italy**-or **California,** for that matter.

EASTER: In many respects, **Easter** is the major occasion of the Greek year. Many Foreigners deliberately time their visit to Greece so as to be able to experience some of the events associated with the **Greek Easter.** Because it does not usually coincide with the **Easter** celebrated in the **Western Christian churches,** care must be taken that you do not arrive at the wrong time. The **Greek Orthodox Easter** is calculated as follows: it must fall after the first full moon following the first day of spring (as is true with **Western Christian Easter**) but it must also fall after the **Jewish Passover.** This then affects the

Lent period-including the two weeks before **Lent** known as Carnival, with its festivities and parades, culminating in **Clean Monday,** with its vegetarian feast and kite-flying. And of course **Good Friday** depends on Easter's date: this is marked by a funeral procession through the streets. Saturday evening involves a church service that ends at midnight with the lighting of candles. **Easter Sunday** itself is an occasion for feasting and festivities. And even the Monday after is observed as a holiday. Ideally you should try to get invited to some village where the traditional **Easter** is observed, but even in the large cities there is enough to make a stranger feel the full impact of Easter on Greeks.

ELECTRICITY: Greece has now converted to A(lternating) C(urrent) at 220 voltage. This means that **Americans** must have converters for their 110-115 volt electrical appliances. Furthermore Greek outlets and plugs vary considerably from both **American** and many **European** standard types, so converters may be required. But electricity is virtually everywhere in Greece.

EMBASSIES: See CONSULATES AND EMBASSIES

EMERGENCIES: For emergency help of any kind, you will get a response 24 hours a day (and hopefully in a language you can speak) by dialing either the **Tourist Police (171)** or the regular police, **(100)** anywhere in Greece. (However, in smaller towns and villages, you will first have to dial the code to the nearest 125 large city). Another possibility is to get to a hotel's reception desk and ask them to make the first call.

FISHING: There is relatively little freshwater fishing in most parts of Greece-and the saltwater fishing in the Mediterranean is not as good as one might assume. But Greeks do catch fish, obviously. No license is required. Nor is any license required for underwater speargun fishing: however, you must be at least 200 meters (667 feet) away from any other people in the water.

FOOD AND DRINK: Whatever else people come to Greece to enjoy, they all spend a fair amount of their time in eating and drinking. And since food and drink end up being among the main ingredients-and usually pleasures-of a Greek holiday, certain things might be said to improve their chances of being enjoyed.

To start with the first meal, breakfast-in most hotels this will be the "continental" type: coffee, possibly some sort of juice, bread, butter, and jelly. Unfortunately, all too often these are less than exciting. If you are required to take breakfast as part of your hotel's rates, that's that. But if you have a choice, you might consider going out and assembling your own breakfast: buying fresh fruit, buying your own roll or cheese pie or sweet, and then taking nothing but coffee in a cafe. Depending on your personal preference, you can take your large dinner at noon or in the evening, as most Greek restaurants offer the same menu, noon and night. (Only the more luxurious restaurants prepare a more elaborate menu for the evening.) But consider: if you intend to move about in the heat of the afternoon, you should probably eat light. Then treat yourself to something refreshing late afternoon. For Greeks eat their evening meal late-anything before 8 PM is considered early. Another variation is to assemble your own picnic for the noon meal-fresh fruits, bread, cheeses, sliced meats or sardines, etc. And when ordering meals in restaurants, you are welcome to go back to the kitchen area to inspect and point out exactly what you want (and don't hesitate to send back anything that is not what you want). If you do not care for much olive oil, indicate that you want little or no **ladhi**. And if you find the food tepid to cold, indicate that you want your food served **zestós**. (If you're lucky, they'll get it as hot as you prefer it).

Greeks like to eat snacks when drinking anything alcoholic. Shrimp, tomato slices, bits of cheese, artichoke leaves - these are known as **mezés** or **mezedákis**; similar hors d'oeuvres as part of a full meal are **orektiká. Mezés** can be had at almost any little cafe or snack place. Sweets and ice cream (**pagotá**) are obtained at special sweethshops and cafés. Traditionally, Greeks go to these places for desserts, which are not available at typical restaurants.

Coffee was not traditionally served at restaurants, either, but now, to satisfy their many foreign patrons, some restaurants have taken to serving coffee. You must specify whether you want **ellenikós kafés** or "American" (or "French") coffee; the latter will usually be powdered coffee, while the former is what is widely known abroad as the Turkish style-a small cup with the muddy coffee taking up about the bottom third of the cup. The sugar is boiled with the coffee and you must specify the degree of sweetness you want: medium is **métrios,** sweet in **glykó,** light is **me olighi,** and no sugar at all is **skétos.** Tea is avialable, too. And Greeks usually take a glass of cold water with everything they eat or dring. Beer is a popular drink-there are several brands brewed in Greece that are quite decent. As for wines, the native Greek wines certainly can't compete with the world's better varieties, but some are adequate. There is first of all a choice between the **retsina**-wines that have been stored in "resinated" barrels and thus have a mild turpentine(!) flavor: not to everyone's taste, but in fact they go well with the Greek menu-and the **aretsinoto** wines. In addition to the usual whites, pinks, and reds, there are sweet dessert wines and quite good Greek brandies. There is also the Greek **oúzo,** made from distilling the crushed mash after the juice has been pressed from the grapes and then adding a slight anisette flavor.

Above all, whether eating or drinking, in fancy restaurants or simple tavernas, everyone should occasionally experiment with some of the different items on the Greek menu. Don't stay in the rut with the same **moussaká** and Greek salad.

See also RESTAURANTS. And for a discussion of special foods and drinks of Crete, see pages 101 - 2 .

GREEK LANGUAGE: The Greek language is far too complex and subtle to even begin to be taught or learned in a book like this. But there are a few basics that can be conveyed. Elsewhere (pages 141) a short list of words and phrases are provided to help the traveler in the more common situations.

The Written language: Most visitors to Greece will have little to do with written Greek except to attempt to read signs, menus, etc. Greek pronunciation is difficult enough so that its finer points could involve long discussions. Here is the alphabet with the English equivalent of the most common sounds so that at least a start can be made on reading Greek.

The Spoken language: Acquiring even the most basic spoken Greek is difficult or not, depending on an individual's skill in picking up a foreign language. But because of the unfamiliar alphabet, many foreigners get easily discouraged: there is not that gratuitous gain that comes from just looking at words in some foreign languages and gradually realizing that you can figure out meanings. Yet anyone should be able to rely on their ear and then try to approximate pronunciations. Greeks are genuinely appreciative of any such efforts. One problem, however, that Greeks have ignoring: their language depends so much on the accent's falling on the precise syllable that this becomes at least as important as the purity of the sound. When in doubt, try shifting the accent until you hit the proper syllable.

The casual traveler need not become concerned about the 127

historical rivalries between the "pure" and demotic spoken Greek: the demotic will be fine for all situations. Likewise, although there are numerous dialects spoken in various parts of Greece-some quite different in pronunciation and vocabulary-the foreigner will be doing fine just to speak a basic Greek. Put another way, dialect variations are the least of a foreigner's problems!

GUIDES AND INTERPRETERS: Officially licensed guides can be provided from the **National Tourist Organization offices** or by the bigger travel agents. Their fees are also officially controlled-and depend on such factors as the time involved, the number in the party, the difficulty of the excursion, etc. Tours organized by travel agencies, of course, usually provide guides who speak the language(s) of the majority of the foreigners taking the tour. If you are lucky, you will get a guide who

HAIRDRESSERS: There are many hairdressers in all large to medium-sized Greek cities. You can get a complete line of services. Tipping is expected-perhaps 10% for the principal hairdresser, half that for the assistant.

HITCHHIKING: As long as basic precautions are observed, hitchhiking (also known to Europeans as "autostop") is generally allowed throughout Greece. Young women, whether alone or in pairs, should exercise special judgment as to the rides they accept.

HOLIDAYS: There are two types of holidays that tourists will want to know about while in Greece. One includes the national holidays when not only all banks, museums archaeological sites, almost all stores, and even many restaurants are closed. These are the following days:

January 1-	New Year's day
January 6-	Epifhany
Last Monday before Lent	
Good Friday	Movable dates (**See** EASTER)
Easter Sunday	
Easter Monday	
March 25	Greek Independence Day
May 1	Spring Festival, or May Day
August 15-	Assumption of the Virgin Mary
October 28-	Okhi (No!) Day
	(Second World War incident)
December 25-	Christmas Day

not only is comfortable with your language but has a true command of the subject-that is, you will get much more than a mechanical-rote recitation of facts.

But it addition to thes national holidays, there ar numerous local holidays and festivals-in honor of som historical or patriotic event, saint, an age-old festival. I particular, "name-days" are major occasions when the saint's name is one of the more popular ones: people with that name often come from great distances to a monastery, chapel, or village where that saint is especially honored. Sometimes Greek festivities go on for two or more days, involving dancing and feasting. Foreigners are traditionally welcomed, and anyone with a taste for such occasions should inquire from the **National Tourist Organization office** or **Tourist Police** - or, for that matter, from almost any Greek who seems informed-about any forthcoming holiday of this kind. See also HOURS, EASTER.

HOSPITALITY: Greek hospitality is legendary, and it usually lives up to its reputation, especially in more remote villages and where only a few foreigners are involved. But in recent years, with the influx of literally millions of foreigners annually, there has inevitably been some pulling back: there is no way that Greeks can "relate to" every single foreigner who crosses paths with them, let alone afford to extend the full panoply of traditional hospitality. However, arrive in a small party in a remote village and you may still be treated as a special guest-offered special drinks and food, presented with little gifts when you leave. Greek males still usually insist on paying for meals when they take a foreigner to a favorite eating place. You will often be offered a coffee or cold drink when visiting with a Greek-and the Greeks present will expect you to accept even as they refuse anything for themselves. But this hospitality works both ways. Greeks in these situations will often question foreigners about fairly personal matters-why a married couple doesn't have children, how much money you have paid for certain items. And once the preliminaries are underway, Greeks expect you to participate to the end: if they have begun to plan a meal for you, they would be genuinely hurt if you ran off to save them the trouble and expense. So don't embark on these encounters unless you are prepared to enjoy them all the way.

HOSPITALS: All large, medium-sized, and even some quite small towns have hospitals or at least clinics. You might go direct to one if you have some medical emergency. Only in the larger cities, of course, could you expect to find a full range of services and specialists. Greek hospitals provide minimal nursing care: a member of the family will often bed down next to the patient to provide full attention, meals, etc. Most foreigners will never have any contact with hospitals, but if you had to you will find that they are quite adequate. See also DOCTORS, EMERGENCIES.

HOSTELS: There are **Youth Hostels** throughout Greece - in most major cities and also in tourist centers. You will almost certainly be asked to produce a membership card from a recognized Youth Hostel association; if you do not have one from your home country, you can join (for a fee) the **Greek Youth Hostels Association** (at 4 Dragatsaniou

Street, Athens). There is usually a limit of 5 days on your stay at these hostels.

HOTELS: There are hotels to suit all tastes and all pocketbooks all over Greece. If you have particular preferences as to price, location, or other specifics, you should reserve in advance for the main tourist season: no one ever spends the night on the street, but you cannot be certain of getting the exact hotel you want. At other times of the year, however, there is generally a surplus of beds. All hotel and room accommodations in Greece are quite strictly controlled-as to price, conditions, etc.-by the government. There are various classes, or categories, of hotels, form Deluxe and then Class A through E; the criteria may not always seem important to all guests (e.g. size of public rooms, telephones in rooms), but in general the categories reflect the levels of amenities. Many tourists find the Class C hotels-most of which are relatively new-quite adequate (and they cost about one-half a Class A hotel and two-thirds a Class B). The prices are supposed to be posted in each room, but sometimes it is hard for a hotel to keep up with all seasonal changes.

Ask for the price of the room before you agree to anything (and then ask to inspect it , if you care to). Find out if the price quoted includes all taxes and whether it includes any meals: hotels are allowed to require clients to take breakfast, if offered by the hotel, and the Class B, A, and Deluxe hotels may also require clients to take at least one other meal if the hotel maintains a dining room. Service charges should be included in the price quoted but you may want to tip a bit extra anyone who has done you any personal favors. Prices may be raised during the "high" tourist season (and may be lowered during the off season); hotels can also charge an extra 10% if you stay less than three nights. It all sounds quite complicated, but in practice you are told a price of a room and that's usually the end of it. Do clarify the various possibilities, however, if you are concerned.

HOURS: Greek shop hours can be a quite complicated subject, but in general stores open at 8 AM and close around 1:30 or 2 PM, Monday through Saturday; on several days a week (but not Saturday) some shops reopen again from about 5 to 8:30 PM. Inquire in the morning if you have any special needs for that day. And of course all shops observe the national holidays. See HOLI-DAYS.

HUNTING: Foreigners may hunt within Greece but only with a license and with limitations on seasons, type of game, etc. There are also limits on the types of weapons and ammunition you can bring in. Inquire at the **National Tourist Organization** or a **Greek Embassy** abroad if this is to be an important part of your visit to Greece.

INFORMATION: There are various sources for detailed information about Greece. Abroad, there are the **Greek Embassies** and **Consulates**; the **National Tourist Organization** maintains offices in many of the principal cities of the world; and travel agents have some types of touristic information. Within Greece, there are the various offices of the **National Tourist Organization**, the **Tourist Police**, and also the travel agencies. One of the problems for all of these offices is to keep up with the many changes from year to year and from season to season in schedules, prices, etc. Thus, not until you actually get to Greece can you probably find out exact times and costs of the sailings to the many Greek islands; what you should be able to learn while still abroad is whether such service is usually available.

LAUNDRY: Laundry can usually be placed at a drycleaning establishment to be picked up within 24 hours, and the better class hotels usually will take care of laundry for their clients. But wherever it is done, it will seem expensive (especially relative to so many other costs in Greece). But every item will be neatly ironed, and in some situations this service may be a necessary expense. There are almost no self-service laundries anywhere in Greece-there has been one in the **Plaka** section of **Athens**. Most tourists simply make do by washing out things in their rooms and then hanging them on the usually present balcony.

LUGGAGE: Greek air terminals and bus stations usually do not provide any place to leave luggage for even short periods of time. Tourists are left to make their own arrangements-with a cafe, restaurant, hotel, store, or wherever. Offer a reasonable sum for the service, and although it cannot be legally guaranteed, your luggage should always be safe.

MEDICINES: See PHARMACIES

MENU: See RESTAURANTS

MONEY: The basic Greek currency is the Drachma. The Lepta-100 make up a Drachmahas all but vanished from common usage, although occasionally prices are quoted with a 50 Lepta. (When Greek shopkeepers or others lack small change, they automatically "round off"-sometimes to your advantage, sometimes to theirs). The exchange rate of the Drachma with various foreign currencies has been fluctuating so in recent years that it would be misleading to provide specific figures here. As soon as you find out the exchange rate for your own national currency, calculate some basic equivalencies-that is, what does 5 Drachmas, equal, 10 Drachmas, 50 Drachmas, etc. This will provide a general sense of what things are costing. Technically you are limited to importing (and exporting) 1,500 Drachmas in currency; most foreigners are never even questioned, let alone inspected, but there is no real "black market" in Greek currency and little opportunity for most people to gain anything by violating the law. See also BANKS.

MOTORBIKES FOR RENT: Motorbikes may be rented from various agents in the main cities and resort centers. Rates vary but they obviously become cheaper over longer periods. During the main tourist season and over

131

holidays, you should probably reserve in advance. To rent a motorbike, however, you must be at least 18 years of age and licensed to operate one. You (and any passengers) must wear a protective helmet. And you should carry all the insurance you can get. See also BICYCLES FOR RENT.

MOUNTAINEERING: It may be overlooked-considering that most people come to Greece to enjoy the beaches and water-that Greece also has many fine mountains that offer challenging and enjoyable possibilities. There is a **Greek Mountainclimbing Club** (EOS is the Greek acronym), with branches in many cities, and foreigners are made to feel welcome on their excursions and in their facilities. They maintain various huts on major mountains. Although the peaks may not seem that high by world standards, the weather conditions often make some of the ascents quite difficult, and certainly no one should set out to climb unless properly equipped and experienced. Consult the **National Tourist Organization** for details about contacting a local mountaineering club or obtaining a local guide.

MOVIES: No one would ever travel to Greece to see a movie-the selection, even in **Athens,** is usually dismal, and in smaller cities it is hard to know where such movies have come from. But there are times when someone might want to retreat to a movie, and during the summer, when there are many outdoor movie theaters, it can be quite pleasant to sit under the starry Mediterranean sky and sit back and enjoy a movie you'd feel guilty about

seeing at home. Most foreign films in Greece are shown in their original language and with Greek subtitles, but ask to make sure before you enter.

NEWSPAPERS AND MAGAZINES: There is a large selection of foreign-language (that is, non-Greek) newspapers and magazines to be found in the large and medium -sized cities and also in all tourist centers. Athens has an English-language daily, **The Athens News,** and a fine English-language monthly, **The Athenian.** There is also a good selection of papers and periodicals brought in from abroad; they tend to be expensive (compared to prices at home)· and the news will seem a bit dated (when you first arrive), but the longer you stay the more you may appreciate these links with the world.

PARKING: There was once a time when there were so few cars that finding a parking place was no problem in Greece. Then came a phase when the car population "exploded" so fast they took over every available sidewalk and corner. Now the Greek police have begun to fight back: in Athens and some cities, the police remove the license plates when your car is in violation and you must go to the local stationhouse and pay the fine to retrieve your plates. Meters are appearing in some cities. Parking restrictions are generally enforced, for foreigners as well as Greeks. Athens and several other cities and tourist centers have set aside a few places for tourist parking (marked by signs) but during the main season these are as hard to find free as any other places.

PASSPORTS AND VISAS: A valid national passport is all that is required of most visitors to Greece-although you will probably be asked to fill out an entry card on the airplane or ship-so long as you are a transient: This period varies (depending on reciprocal arrangements with the individual's home country), but for **British** and **Commonwealth** subjects this is three months and for **Americans,** two months. For longer stays, visas must be applied for: Inquire at the **Tourist Police** or **National Tourist Organization** as to how to proceed.

PENSIONS: These are a cheaper, more basic type of accommodation to be found in locales where a lot of travelers pass through. You probably won't have a private toilet or bath, and the buildings will usually be older, but linen will be clean and some people prefer the more homey atmosphere. Breakfast is usually available at a pension. See also ROOMS TO RENT.

PHARMACIES: Pharmacies, drugstores, or chemists, there are plenty of them around Greece and they carry a fairly full selection of prescription drugs as well as general health, sanitary, and cosmetic items. (A pharmacy is usually clearly marked by a **red Maltese cross.**) There will always be at least one pharmacy open, 24 hours a day, in any large city: the closed ones should have a sign in their window indicating which one is open. If you have special medical needs, of course, you had better make arrangements with your own doctor at home before setting off.

PHOTOGRAPHY: Greece is famed as a photographer's paradise, what with its light and subjects. There are plenty of shops selling films and camera supplies-but all are expensive and you are advised to bring your own. You can get your films developed in relatively short times. In traveling about Greece, be careful to observe the occasional restrictions against photographing in areas of military bases.

POLICE: See EMERGENCIES

POST OFFICE: Any good-sized city will have its post office, and larger cities will have several branch offices. They keep varied hours, but best is to get there in the morning. Some will open for only limited service in the late afternoon-postage stamps or for **Poste Restante.** (This latter refers to mail addressed to someone with no other known or fixed address-what Americans know as **General Delivery.**) Postage rates vary considerably (and rise inevitably) depending on the nature of the item (post card, letter, etc.), the weight, the destination, etc. The best is to know the basic stamps for most of your mail (that is, air mail post cards to your homeland, the lightest air mail letters, etc.) and be prepared to have any mail in question weighed. Stamps can often be purchased at certain stationery shops but you will pay a slight surcharge for the privilege.

PRICES: The one thing certain is that they will rise over time, in Greece as else-
133

where. Some prices, however, do come down during the off-season-hotels in particular. By and large, prices are well marked for most items you will be purchasing, whether food in the market, or clothes in a store, and Greeks do not appreciate your trying to negotiate prices. If a shopkeeper sees you about to leave he may make some kind of a reduction or offer, but he does not want you to turn every purchase into a bazaar haggling.

RADIO: There are several possibilities for foreigners who like to keep up with the news via radio and in their own language. Greek stations provide at least one brief program daily with news and weather in **English, French,** and **German.** The American Armed Forces Radio broadcasts 24 hours daily, with frequent news updates. And there is the **BBC** overseas and the **Voice of America.**

REDUCTIONS: There are some reductions in admissions to museums and archaeological sites but they are limited to special groups. Foreign students of subjects directly related to the world of Greek art and archaeology can get a pass that allows for a 50% reduction to all national sites and museums (not to locally run). Students who present an **International Student Identity Card** are granted a reduced fee at some places. And a very special group of archaeologists, professors of art and architecture and classical subjects, museum professionals, **UNESCO** and some other government officials are given free entry to sites and muse-

ums. If you think you qualify, go to the **Directorate of Antiquities,** 14 Aristidou St., Athens, with proper identification and find out how to comply.

RELIGION: See CHURCHES

RESTAURANTS: There is no problem in finding a restaurant in Greece, and although they range from the quite elaborate and expensive to the rather dingy and cheap, most foreigners end up patronizing a relatively narrow spectrum. They are officially classed, and this affects the prices they are allowed to charge. The easy way to approach a restaurant is to make sure its appearance appeals and then look at some standard item on the menu-which should always be posted out front-and see how its price compares with the same item in other places you've eaten in. Not necessarily, but usually, if the moussaka or Greek salad is expensive, then everything will be expensive. Once you have decided to eat there, go to the kitchen area and select your foods-most proprietors are happy to have you do so; this eliminates the need for a lot of talking and the possibility of some unwanted surprises. Send back food if it is not what you want. The standard printed Greek menu has its prices listed in two columns: that on the left is the price before the obligatory service charge, that on the right includes the service percentage-and it is the latter you will be billed for. It is customary, even so, to tell the waiter to keep a small extra sum when he presents the change; and if there was a "waterboy" for your table you leave a few Drachmas for him.

ROOMS TO RENT: In some of the more crowded tourist centers individual families have taken to renting rooms in their homes. They are supposed to be supervised so that basic sanitary practices are observed, no matter how simple the accommodation. They are relatively cheap and many people find such rooms adequate. See also PENSIONS

SAILING: See YACHTS

SHOESHINE: In the larger cities, young boys or even men will be shining shoes in various public areas. Agree on the price beforehand-and if you are in doubt, ask a Greek to help establish the cost. A small tip is customary.

SHOPPING AND SOUVENIRS: In the largest and even in relatively small cities of Greece, you will be able to purchase almost any item you need for your stay in Greece. Often as not it will even be your favorite brand, since Greeks import virtually everything: your favorite suntan lotion, your preferred instant coffee-they'll probably be available. But these are not what most people come to Greece to buy. It is the souvenirs and specialties of Greece that interest most travelers, and here the selection is almost overwhelming, especially in the major tourist centers. Since everyone's taste differs as to what constitutes a suitable souvenir, there is no use laying down rules. Take your time and look around: it is not that shops cheat but simply that prices often will be lower in one place than another-and sometimes the lowest price will be in some unexpected location. (Even then, the difference may be relatively few Drachmas, so you must ask yourself how much of your limited time you want to spend in comparison shopping.) It is difficult to find genuine handmade artifacts, but they are available, and often not that much more expensive than the massproduced items. Often it is the smaller and less centrally located shops that have the unusual items, so leave the main streets lined with gift shops and go looking. Even then, don't give too much credence to claims of age or uniqueness or "the last one left...": just buy what you like at the price you feel you want to pay. See also PRICES and HOURS.

SPORTS: Those who like to include active sports in their vacations and travels will find many opportunities to do so in Greece. In the winter, for instance, there are several ski lifts operating (most of them in central and northern Greece, but one in the White Mountains of Crete). There are several golf clubs in Greece (near **Athens,** and on **Rhodes** and **Corfu**). There is horseback riding (at Athens, Salonica, and on Crete). Several of the major resort hotels offer waterskiing, and many public beaches now have paddleboats and surfsails for rent. And Greek youths can usually be found playing informal games of soccer (football) or basketball: if you ask, you could probably join in. See also Mountaineering, Swimming, Tennis, Underwater Sports, Yachting.

135

SWIMMING: Swimming- or at least sunbathing is perhaps the main attraction for many visitors to Greece, and there are almost limitless beaches. In fact, though, not all Greek beaches are as sandy as you might wish. Inquire if you have a strong preference and a choice as to where the sandy beach is located. Likewise, not all beaches are as clean as you might wish- although if you get away from a city or built-up area the water should be perfectly clean and clear. What you cannot always escape-anywhere in the Mediterranean - is the tar that washes ashore and gets into the sand: a beach may look perfectly clean. but as you walk along the sand your feet pick up the buried tar. (This is one reason many people have taken to bringing flexible mats to the beaches: to save their towels from getting fouled). The usual precautions about avoiding undertows and un-expected currents should be observed. Many cities operate public beach facilities-changing rooms, showers, etc. Nudist beaches are officially forbidden and in some areas local individuals actively seek to enforce the ban; in some places, if it is done with discretion, it will be ignored. Lastly the Mediterranean is not the tropics, and most people find the swimming season lasts only from May through September.

TAXIS: Taxis remain relatively cheap in Greece. They can also be hard to hire during certain busy hours-and for that reason, Greeks often share taxis, each party paying the metered fare to their destination. There is a minimum fare, too-no matter how short the distance. There may also be some surcharges beyond the metered fare: for night rides, for certain holidays, for luggage, to airports, etc. (Drivers should be able to indicate any such surcharges.) If it is to be an especially long trip, negotiate the fee before leaving. If it is to a remote locale and you want the driver to wait, there are set fees for waiting time. With two or more individuals sharing the cost, a taxi offers a reasonable way to make best use of a limited time in Greece.

TELEPHONES AND TELEGRAMS: In a few large cities, it has been traditional to use the phones available at many kiosks (or **peripterons**); you dial first and after you have completed your call you pay the proprietor. Now a large red telephone is replacing this system-and you must insert the coin first (it has for some time been a two-Drachma coin). Increasingly, too, phone booths are appearing all over Greece, and for these you need a two - Drachma coin. In some special phone booths you can even dial long distance, but most foreigners (as do most Greeks) will prefer to go to the office of the national phone company (**OTE**) and use the attended services. If you know-or can learn-the code numbers for your desired call, you can dial direct to virtually any place in the world. (Be persistent, though: the Greek phone system is good, but you must often try dialing several times to make your connection). When you are finished with your call, you step over to the attendant who will read the meter and provide you with a "bill". Since many Greeks still do not have telephones, these offices can be quite crowded at certain times, so go well in advance if you must place a call within a set period. Telegrams are sent from these same offices. The forms are printed in English as well as Greek, and the attendants are usually adept at dealing with foreigners' queries. Large hotels might be able to help you, too, with any special problems.

TENNIS: There are a fair number of tennis courts around Greece and most are open to non-Greeks (and non-members of the sponsoring clubs). Naturally the courts tend to be concentrated in a few areas-Athens (and its nearby beach resorts), large cities such as **Salonika** and **Patras,** and in the more popular holiday centers such as Crete, Rhodes, and Corfu. Inquire at offices of the **National Tourist Organization** for details; if tennis is a vital part of your holiday in Greece, you should make certain of arrangements before going to a particular locale.

THEFT: This is virtually a non-existent problem in Greece. Luggage can be left unattanded almost anywhere, purses or cameras can be forgotten at a restaurant-you will always find them waiting for you. On the other hand, it would be silly to leave a lot of currency or small valuables (jewels, watches, etc.) lying around in your hotel room: there are simply too many people passing through.

TIME: Greece is two hours ahead of **Greenwich Mean Time** (that is, **London's** time).

Greece now observes **Summer Time** (in which clocks are set one hour ahead) on the same schedule as its fellow **Common Market** members. As for time during the Greek day, Greeks do not concern themselves much with punctuality. Beyond that, when they say "tomorrow morning", they may mean at 12 noon; "this afternoon" may well mean 4 PM. Make a fixed appointment, by all means, but do not get excited if it isn't kept to the minute.

TIPPING: Greeks used to consider it as beneath their dignity to accept tips, but the influx of foreign tourists has changed all that. Even so, by including the service charges in restaurant bills and hotel bills, Greeks try to eliminate some of the awkwardness involved in tipping. It is customary to give the waiter at least some "rounded off" change (e.g. the 15 Drachmas over a 385 Drachma bill); coins left on the table will go to the waterboy if there has been one. If you have had some personal contact or asked special services of personnel in your hotel, it is certainly not out of line to present a tip. Barbers, hairdressers, shoes-hiners, and ushers (in movies as well as theaters) traditionally get modest tips. Taxi drivers are not supposed to expect tips, but you can expect a less than gracious smile if you do not at least give a small sum over the fare.

TOILETS: Hotels that most foreigners now stay in have modern toilet facilities (although the plumbing may look a bit exotic). Many of the older restaurants and taver-137

nas, however, have quite primitive toilets: if you are squeamish about this, use your hotel toilet before going out to eat. There are public toilets (the attendants expect a tip) in all medium sized to large Greek cities-but they are often fairly primitive, too. Most of the better hotels have separate toilet facilities for their patrons, and if you look as though you belong you can usually make use of them.

TRAVELERS CHECKS: All the better known travelers checks are honored in banks, hotels, restaurants that cater to foreigners, and tourist gift shops. Do not expect every little corner store or village taverna, however, to accept a travelers check: buy your Drachmas before setting off for the countryside. See also CREDIT CARDS and BANKS.

UNDERWATER SPORTS: SCUBA diving is generally forbidden in Greek waters-the exception being in certain areas and under some supervision. (This restriction is because the Greeks fear that too many divers could lead to losses of their antiquities still to be found around the coasts.) Inquire at the National Tourist Organization for specifics. However, snorkeling (that is, with just a breathing tube, mask, and flippers) is allowed (as is fishing with a speargun, so long as it is not close to swimmers: See FISHING).

VILLAS FOR RENT: It is relatively easy-if expensive!-to rent completely furnished villas in many of the more popular holiday locales a-round Greece. (Villas, by the way, are distinguished from "houses" in that the former usually are out of the main residential areas and usually have a bit of land). Many villas are now rented only through various travel agents or firms specializing in such rentals: inquire of the National Tourist Organization or of major travel agents. Villas can be very expensive during the main season, but if several people are sharing the cost and make a fair number of meals at home, a villa can end up being relatively cheap.

VISAS: See PASSPORTS AND VISAS

WATER: The water of Greece is safe to drink in virtually any place the average traveler will be. (If foreigners sometimes complain of minor stomach ailments when traveling in Greece, it probably is not the water; in any case, it may be little more than a shift from one water to another-the type of upset one could experience in moving from any city to another). The fresh cold water from a natural spring is one of the delights of Greece. If you are truly sensitive, of course, you can always drink bottled water. A more realistic problem might be to get hot water whenever you want it in your hotel: ask beforehand to find out if hot water is provided at only certain hours.

YACHTING: There are numerous firms that rent yachts-mostly with crews - and this has become a popular way to tour Greece. They are undoubtedly expensive at first hearing, but if the cost is divided among several people, and then hotels, other transportation, and at least some meals are being eliminated, the end result is not that expensive. These yachts come in all sizes, with or without sail, and with greater or lesser degrees of luxury. Inquire of the National Tourist Organization or major travel agents for more details.

YOUTH HOSTELS: SEE HOSTELS

ZOOS: For those people who like to round out their view of a foreign land by visiting the local zoo, Greece offers nothing truly worthy of that name. Athens, however, does have a modest display of animals in the National Garden, and it offers the advantage of being central and a convenient retreat from the heat and bustle of the city. And many Greek cities maintain small collections of animals in their public parks-often including some of the less familiar species of Greece such as the famous wild goat of Crete. Inquire of the local **Tourist Police** if you enjoy such diversions.

8. A little Greek for travelers

A	α	(álfa)	As in far.
B	β	(víta)	Closer to a soft v than to b.
Γ	γ	(gámma)	Before a, o, u: **gh**. Before e, i: **y**.
Δ	δ	(dhélta)	Closer to **dh** than to hard **d**.
E	ε	(épsilon)	As in sell.
Z	ζ	(zíta)	As in zeal.
H	η	(íta)	As in machine.
Θ	θ	(thíta)	As in theater.
I	ι	(jóta)	As in machine.
K	κ	(káppa)	As in kit.
Λ	λ	(lámdha)	As in lamp.
M	μ	(mí)	As in mit.
N	ν	(ní)	As in not.
Ξ	ξ	(xí)	As **ks** sound (as in extra)
O	ο	(ómikron)	As in oar.
Π	π	(pí)	As in pit.
P	ρ	(ró)	As in red.
Σ	σ	ç(sígma)	As in sit.
T	τ	(táf)	As in tap.
Y	υ	(ípsilon)	As in machine.
Φ	φ	(fí)	As in fish.
X	χ	(chí)	A **kh** sound (as in **Khan**).
Ψ	ψ	(psí)	A **ps** sound (as in **apse**).
Ω	ω	(oméga)	As in ode.

BASIC DAILY SITUATIONS

Yes	né
Yes indeed!	málista
No	óchi
Greetings!	chérete!
Good morning	kaliméra
Good evening	kalispéra
Good night	kaliníkta
Stay well!	sto kaló
Excuse me	me sinchoríte **or** signómi!
Please	parakaló
Thank you	efcharistó
Not at all	típota
How are you	Ti kánete? **or** pos páte?
Very well	polí kalá
Do you speak English?	Miláte angliká?
I don't understand	Dhen katalavéno
What is that called?	Pos to léne aftó?
How do you say that in Greek?	Pos to léne aftó sta ellhniká?
What is your name?	Pos sas léne?
My name is-	Me léne- .
Mister	kírios
Mrs.	kiría
Child	pedhí
Much	polí
Little	lígho
Over	epáno
Under	káto
There	ekí
Here	edó
Big	megálos
Little	mikrós

NUMBERS

1	éna	18	dhekaoktó
2	dhío	19	dhekaenéa
3	tría	20	íkossi
4	téssara	21	ikosiéna
5	pénte	30	triánda
6	éxi	40	saránda
7	eftá	50	penínda
8	októ	60	exínda
9	enéa	70	evdomínta
10	dhéka	80	ogdhónda
11	éndheka	90	enenínda
12	dódheka	100	ekató
13	dhekatría	200	diakóssia

142

14 dhekatéssera	300 triakóssia
15 dhekapénde	1000 khília
16 dhekaéxi	2000 dhío khiliádes
17 dhekaeftá	

TIME

Morning	to proí
Midday	to messiméri
Afternoon	to apóyevma
Evening	to vrádhi
Night	i níkhta
Yesterday	chtés
Today	símera
Tomorrow	ávrio
Early	enorís
Late	argá
When?	Póte?
Four o'clock (AM)	Stis tésseres to proí
At 5:30 PM	Stis pendémisi to apóyevma
Sunday	Kiriakí
Monday	Dheftéra
Tuesday	Tríti
Wednesday	Tetárti
Thursday	Pémpti
Friday	Paraskeví
Saturday	Sávato
Hour	óra
Day	iméra
Week	evdhomádha
Month	mínas
Year	chrónos

HOTEL

Hotel	xenodhokhío
Room	dhomátio
Bathroom	bánio
Bed	kreváti
Cover	kouvérta
Pillow	maxilári
Lamp	lámba
Cold water	krío neró
Hot water	zestó neró
Key	klidhí
Guest	xénos
Do you have a room with 2 beds?	Échete éna dhíklino dhomátio?
I am staying only one night	Tha míno mía níkhta

143

| Can I pay with a credit card? | Boró na pliróso me aftí ti pistotikí káfta? |
| Do you accept travelers' checks? | Pérnete travellers checks? |

RESTAURANTS

Restaurant	estiatório
Food	fayitó
Table	trapézi
Chair	karékla
Napkin	petséta
Plate	piáto
Cup	flitzáni
Glass	potíri
Fork	piroúni
Spoon	koutáli
Knife	machéri
Waiter	garsóni
Waterboy	mikrós
Check	loghariasmós
Tip	pourboire
Menu	katáloghos
Hors d'oeuvres	orektiká
Bread	psomí
Water	neró
Wine	krassí
Beer	bíra
Milk	ghála
Meat	kréas
Fish	psária
Chicken	kotópoulo
Hot	zestós
Cold	kríos

AROUND TOWN

Street	othós
Square	platía
Boulevard	leofóros
Attention!	Prossochí!
Forbidden	Apaghorévete
Open	aniktós
Shut	klistós
Entrance	íssodhos
Exit	éxodhos
Toilet	toualéta
Women	ghynekón
Men	andhrón
Store	maghazí
Kiosk	períptero

post office	takhidhromío
letter	ghrámma
stamp	grammatósimo
airmail	aeroporikós
telephone	tiléfono
telegram	tilegráfima
How much does it cost?	Póso káni aftó?
bank	trápeza
money	khrímata
drachmas	drachmés
I would like to exchange a check	Thélo na aláxo éna tsek.
laundry	plidirio
dry-cleaning	katharistírio
I need it tommorow	Prépi na íne étimo ávrio to proí

ON THE ROAD

automobile	aftokínito
bus	leoforío
taxi	taxi
motorcycle	motosikléta
bicycle	podhílato
ship	plío **or** karávi
airplane	aeropláno
railroad station	stathmós trénou
stop(bus)	stássi
map	khártis
ticket	issitírio
Gas station	pratírion venzínis
Gas	venzíni
Oil	ládhi
Kilometer	khiliómetro
straight ahead	kat efthían
Right	dhexiá
Left	aristerá
Opposite	apénandi
One way	apló
Roundtrip (return)	me epistrofí
Quickly	grígora
Slowly	sighá
Where is-?	Pou íne?-
How many hours?	Pósses óres?
When does the bus leave?	Ti óra févyi to leoforío?

INDEX

148